PRESENT

Any At-
tion Will
Arrest.

KILL SIX
BURN NE...

Search for Accused Negro Con- ADVOCATES
Leads to Rate That in
New Die. Albany Streets

FRIDAY EVENING, JANUA

proved
sale
of the
large re-
gen-
but
things
to
in
the
not
their

the

WHITES GATHER
FOR MILES TO
SLAY NEGROES

W YORK TIMES.

LAST NEGRO HOMES
RAZED IN ROSEWOOD

Florida M.t Deliberately Fires
Another

MW01526953

HOW WHITE RACISTS WIPED A BLACK TOWN OFF THE MAP

VANISHED

BY DAVID GELIEBTER

———

Dedicated to
Marga Nelson

———

CONTENTS

Introduction   9

Chapter 1   **America's Original Sin**   15

Chapter 2   **Devil in A White Hood**   47

Chapter 3   **Raise Up The Devil**   73

Chapter 4   **Rosewood Massacre**   95

Chapter 5   **Aftermath**   123

Chapter 6   **Afterword**   153

Chapter 7   **Sources**   157

About the Author   163

INTRODUCTION

> *"They went
> to killin'
> everything—
> babies and all.
> Dogs, cats—
> everything."*
>
> —ROSEWOOD RESIDENT

In the early 1920s, Sumner, Florida was a secluded mill town in the northeastern corner
of the state, just below the Panhandle.

Florida's population of about a half a million
was split evenly along racial lines—with little
mixing of Whites and "Coloreds."

Sumner was a "white town." Blacks lived
one community over, in Rosewood. Both were
part of a single voting district in Levy County. The U.S. Census listed a combined
638 inhabitants—294 Whites and 344 Blacks.

Many residents from both Sumner and Rosewood worked for Cummer and Sons
Cypress, a logging and mill operation. The company had relocated from Michigan
when the standing timber was exhausted, acquiring 117,000 acres of Florida woodlands in 1890.

The northern part of the state was blessed with a natural abundance of 100-year-
old virgin cypress trees—the same species as the great sequoias and redwoods of
the West—which, because of their strong, splinter-resistant properties, were ideal
for manufacturing lead pencils, By the turn of the twentieth century, Americans were
going through 240,000 pencils a day.

Long leaf pine trees, so common to the area, were turned into wood "flitches"
for citrus crates. In the 1500s, Spanish explorer Ponce de Leon planted the first

orange trees around St. Augustine, Florida. Count Odet Phillipe, the nephew of French King Louis XVI, brought grapefruit to what is now Tampa in 1823. By the 1920s, the citrus industry was shipping seven million crates of their precious fruit to northern markets each year.

★

The average Cummer mill worker earned $17.00 for a 62-hour work week (just over 27¢ an hour), paid, in part, with scrip that could be used at the company store (a loaf of bread was a dime and a half gallon of milk was 30¢).

Reflecting the paternalism most company towns possessed, the mill provided lodging for its workers. Housing consisted of small, crowded quarters, lit by kerosene lamps. Many had no bathrooms or indoor plumbing. Rent was 50 cents per week. Electricity was 5 cents extra.

Ernest Parham was twelve when he and his family moved from Cedar Keys in 1916, after his father, a logger, "took tuberculosis" and died. Cummer hired Ernest's mother and stepfather to run the only hotel in Sumner.

"Sumner was strictly a sawmill town," he said. "It had a post office, two grocery stores, a barber shop, the hotel, and that was about it."

Though Blacks and Whites worked alongside one another, their lives were spent apart. "My mother, she had this black cook who had a son," notes Parham. "We played with him, but that was it. We never played with the black kids from the quarters. We called them 'ni*ras,' and if you were upset with them, you called them 'N*****s.'"

★

James and Frances Taylor were fortunate to live in one of the company-owned bungalows in Sumner built for the White families—rows of cottages nestled among a network of earthen roads winding through thickets of spindly trees and overgrown bush, flanked by woods and the swamps beyond.

The modestly-furnished, neat-as-a-pin, four-room whitewashed home had cold-running water in the back-porch sink and a wood stove. Ice was delivered free from the mill twice a week.

Frances Jane Coleman Taylor—everybody called her Fannie—was only 15 years old when, in 1917, she married James, six years her senior. They had a 4-year-old boy, Berness, and a 2-month-old infant, Addis Donald.

Fannie's appearance was ordinary—about five foot six, rather bony, her mousy brown hair framed against cheekbones that sat high on her expressionless face.

She was a quiet person. Neighbors described her as somewhat aloof and "very peculiar." She was meticulously clean, scrubbing her cedar floors with bleach so that they shone alabaster white.

"She didn't have nothing to do with anybody," said a resident. Deep in the Bible Belt, she was conspicuously absent from Sunday church, noted several wives.

Fannie's husband, James, was a likeable enough young man—calm, friendly, and easy to get along with. He had a lanky build, big ears, deep brown eyes, and a tanned, freckled complexion.

He worked at the mill oiling the machinery each morning—coaxing the giant whirling contraptions back to life—before workers arrived.

In the short winter days, he left for work when it was still pitch black and deathly silent—except for the crackle of twigs and leaves underfoot. No sounds of "*purr-rreeeek*" from the frogs or incessant buzz of insects, unlike the spirited summer serenades.

★

The ground that New Year's morning was hardened by an unforgiving cold, the listless sky outlined by a majestic panorama of tightly-knit treetops fighting to block beams of sunlight from streaming in.

Leaden grey smoke in the distance meant the men were well into their workday; the sweet scent of freshly-cut cypress permeated the thick air—when the hush was shattered by bloodcurdling screams that sounded like a terrified soul dying.

As wives in their muted frocks and tatty housecoats hurriedly gathered outside, 22-year-old Fannie stood barefoot in front of her house in a simple cotton print dress, dazed, feet unsteady, hair ruffled, her fingers distorted from her muscles going rigid, a nasty purplish bruise revealing itself against her soft pastel cheek.

A Black man, Fannie insisted, had assaulted her.

"Someone needs to grab up my babies!" she hollered, adding, "That N*****'s still here!"

With that, Fannie fainted.

A neighbor, Francis Smith, whose husband, C.C. Smith, was an oiler at the mill—large pistol in hand—gathered her nerves, yanked open the front door, ran in and scooped up both children and then ran back out.

Whoever assaulted Fannie was gone.

By mid-morning Levy County Sheriff Robert Elisha Walker—with his owlish school teacher looks—had assembled a posse of a dozen men, most still in their mill work denims and farmer jeans.

The sheriff had the presence of mind to secure a few bloodhounds from a nearby prison work camp.

Suspicion quickly fell on Jesse Hunter, a Black convict who had escaped from a nearby chain gang doing road construction near Otter Creek.

No negro was going to attack a White woman. Those coloreds needed to learn themselves a lesson. No way was this going to happen again to another innocent White girl.

★

Only weeks before, in nearby Perry, a comely, 26-year-old White schoolteacher, Ruby Hendry, was found by a railroad crew lying dead—in a pool of blood—near the train tracks. It took half an hour to identify the body because her "blood-stained" face was unrecognizable.

She had been brutally beaten with a blunt instrument. Her throat was cut "in such a horrible manner that death must have been instantaneous." Newspapers also reported that $14.00 was missing from her purse.

The murder of the daughter of a prominent White family (her father was alderman and county tax collector), made this a top priority. Search parties—numbering well over three hundred citizens—were formed and quickly moved in "every direction" to find the killer.

"Through the woods you could hear the dogs," noted Ms. H. U. Baskins, who worked for Ruby Hendry's sister, Hattie Miller. "[My family] sat up all night. Daddy had us all out there on the porch listening at the dogs running."

Even though items found near the dead girl's body belonged to a local White man, police were convinced the perpetrator had to be Black. After six days, Sheriff Lipscomb and Chief Parker arrested a local Black man, Charles Wright, a 21-year-old sawmill operator who lived in Perry with his wife and two children. Albert Young, an escaped convict from Kindlon, Georgia and an acquaintance of Wright's, was also locked up.

When the sheriff attempted to move the prisoners to Taylor County, a White mob estimated at 3,000 to 5,000 formed a "human barrier" and seized Wright. They tortured him, attempting to extract a confession. He refused to name any names, so they burned him alive at the stake.

Ms. Baskins witnessed it: "They had him standing and that chain around him and all that wood, that cord of wood and turpentine poured over it. And he asked him [if] anybody have any word to say. And this lady was pregnant and she walked up close as she could get and spit on him before they threwed that match and burnt him up … The skin off of his head popped like a pistol."

Four days later, the lynch mob attacked again, this time as officers were moving Arthur Young to another jail. He was abducted, his body riddled with bullets, and his corpse left hanging from a tree on the side of a highway. A local Black church, school, Masonic lodge, amusement park and several homes were torched for good measure.

★

William Hathcox, a grizzled mill worker and neighbor of the Taylors, was sick and tired of standing around waiting—as were many in the posse. "That N***** done raped her!" he screeched. "What are we waitin' fer? Let's go get 'em!"

With that, the chase was on.

For the whole of the week, a rampaging, out-of-control mob of White vigilantes—along with an army of Klansmen—would reign terror, death and destruction down on Rosewood.

Virtually every structure in town would be burned to the ground. Afterwards, Rosewood would no longer exist. It would literally vanish from the face of the earth—like it was never there.

The "official" death toll stood at eight: six Blacks and two Whites. Unofficially, many more lost their lives.

Despite widespread coverage in both Black and White newspapers, it wasn't long before the incident slipped from the public's consciousness.

Most survivors scattered to the four winds, never to return—except through the ghastly images that would haunt them in their sleep.

★

What follows, then, is the story of the Rosewood Massacre, "a wilderness paradise felled by an apocalypse of White rage."

It's also a cautionary tale about how structural racism, if left unchecked, can become a cancer on the land.

★

CHAPTER ONE
AMERICA'S ORIGINAL SIN

"Were you a slave when you were called? Don't let it trouble you— although if you can gain your freedom, do so."

—CORINTHIANS 7:21

The history of slavery and racism can be traced back to the beginnings of recorded time.

The Bible stipulates the treatment of slaves, especially in the Old Testament.

In the Christian Bible, Genesis 9:18-27, Ham finds Noah drunk and naked. He tells his brothers, Shem and Japheth, who proceed to cover their father without gazing at him. When Noah finds out what happened, he curses Ham's son Canaan, saying he shall be "a servant of servants."

Jews believe that God dictated the Torah to Moses on Mount Sinai 50 days after their exodus from Egyptian slavery.

There also are references to slavery in the New Testament.

The Qur'an, which Muslims believe to have been revealed by God to the Prophet Muhammad in the seventh century, makes numerous references to slaves and slavery.

★

In August 1619, the *White Lion*, an English privateer commanded by John Jope, dropped anchor at an inlet in the James River at Point Comfort, following a dreadful 10,000-nautical-mile voyage. It was a year before the *Mayflower* would set sail for the New World.

While many Native American tribes practiced some form of slavery long before the Europeans conquered this new land, only to become enslaved themselves by these foreign invaders, it was the introduction of Africans that is generally regarded as the origin of slavery in North America.

They were Kimbundu-speaking peoples from the kingdom of Ndongo, located in part of present-day Angola. Sold by African warlords and mercenaries allied to their Portuguese occupiers, the slave traders forced their captives to march several hundred miles to the coast to board the *San Juan Bautista*, one of several transatlantic slave ships.

The ship set sail with about 350 souls on board, packed in like sardines, wallowing in their waste, the only ventilation a porthole or two. One-third would succumb to starvation and sickness during the Middle Passage. As the ship approached what is now Veracruz, Mexico, it was intercepted by the *White Lion*, along with its sister ship, the *Treasurer*. Dividing the human cargo, the *White Lion* sailed for Virginia.

The colonist John Rolfe wrote to Sir Edwin Sandys of the Virginia Company that a "Dutch man of war" arrived in the colony and "brought not anything but 20 and odd Negroes, which the governor [Sir George Yeardley] and a cape merchant bought for victuals."

Sales at that time were cash or barter, with credit sometimes extended. During the 1600s, a slave sold for $120 to $180 (about $5,000 - $7,500 today).

The Africans were most likely put to work in the tobacco fields that had recently been established in the area. They would work alongside the colony's many White indentured servants.

Thanks to a cheap source of labor, tobacco exports—almost exclusively from the Chesapeake colonies (Virginia, Maryland, and the northeast corner of North Carolina)—surged from 20,000 pounds in 1619 to 38 million pounds in 1700.

★

The *White Lion's* sister ship, *Treasurer,* arrived in Virginia four days later with the remaining captured Africans. One was a young Black slave named Angela, who would become the first African woman documented in Virginia.

She is listed in the 1624 and 1625 census as living in the household of Capitan William Pierce, first as "Angelo a Negar," and then as "Angela Negro woman in by Treasurer."

By then, she had survived two other harrowing events: a Powhatan Indian attack in 1622 that left 347 colonists dead and the famine that followed, which almost wiped out Jamestown.

Angela's arrival coincided with another milestone in American history: the meeting of the first General Assembly in Jamestown's newly built wooden church. The legislative body was made up of the governor, his four councilors and 22 burgesses elected by every free White male settler in the colony.

"It is a great irony," James Horn, president of the Jamestown Rediscovery Foundation said, "that American slavery and democracy were created at the same time and place."

★

The slave trade provided those at the top with political power, social standing, and wealth. Immense money was made in slave trading and by trading the commodities produced by slavery. A number of celebrated and respected families on both sides of the Atlantic made their fortunes from the sinful business.

At the time of his death in 1732 at the age of 69, land baron Robert "King" Carter was the richest man in Virginia. He held at least 295,000 acres of land. His 390 slaves of working age were scattered across 48 properties. Carter's political power, stolen wealth, greed, and imperious bearing earned him the nickname of "King" from his contemporaries.

It was a different story for slaves. They were powerless, regarded as subhuman, worthless except as workhorses of labor. For most, their legacy would be a life of misery and suffering. About the only nickname a slave could be expected to earn is "ni**a."

As Olaudah Equiano, from Benin Kingdom (present-day Nigeria), who was kidnapped and forced into slavery at the age of 11, but who later bought his freedom and became an author and abolitionist, said, "Is it not enough that we are torn from our country and friends, to toil for your luxury and lust of gain? Must every tender feeling be likewise sacrificed to your avarice?"

★

The Middle Passage usually took six to eight weeks, but bad weather could increase it to 12 weeks or more. During that entire time, these hapless souls were crammed into the ship's belly with coarse metal restraints around the arms and legs cutting into their skin.

"The iron entered into our souls," lamented a formerly enslaved man named Caesar.

The lack of sanitation and suffocating conditions—packed so close, many couldn't get to the toilet buckets, forced to lay in their own feces—meant there was a constant threat of disease. Epidemics of fever, dysentery, and smallpox were frequent.

Olaudah Equiano remembered, "I was soon put down under the decks, and there I received such a salutation in my nostrils as I had never experienced in my life: so that, with the loathsomeness of the stench, and crying together, I became so sick and low that I was not able to eat, nor had I the least desire to taste anything. I now wished for the last friend, death, to relieve me."

Women and children were kept in separate quarters, sometimes on deck, but this also exposed them to violence and sexual abuse from the crew.

Children made up a quarter of the captives. Because governments determined by the ton how many people could be fitted onto a slave ship, children were considered especially advantageous—they could fill the boat's small spaces, allowing more human capital in the cargo hold.

On average, some 15 percent of slaves died before they ever reached land. The dead were thrown overboard. Suicide attempts were so common that many captains placed netting around their ships to prevent loss of human cargo and therefore profit.

Enslaved people did not meekly accept their fate. One out of 10 slave ships experienced some form of resistance, including mutiny.

★

Slavery came to America's shores much earlier than 1619. Christopher Columbus likely transported the first Africans to the Americas in the late 1490s on his expeditions to Hispaniola, now part of the Dominican Republic (which included captured indigenous peoples, too).

Significant numbers of African slaves were brought to Spanish-occupied Florida as early as 1526. That year, some became part of an expedition to establish an outpost in San Miguel de Gualdape, in what is now Georgia. The colony was abandoned the following year after a slave revolt.

By 1540, 30,000 African slaves had been sent to the European colonies in the Caribbean, and more than 100,000 were shipped to all of the Americas.

Enslaved Africans may have been on board Sir Francis Drake's fleet when he arrived at Roanoke Island in 1586 in his failed attempt to establish the first permanent English settlement in America.

★

Before African slaves ever arrived on American shores in any numbers, colonists tried exploiting indigenous tribes.

When Jamestown was established, at first the natives were glad to trade provisions with the colonists for metal hatchets and copper, but by 1609 the English governor, John Smith, had begun to send raiding parties to demand food. When the Native Americans fought back, the English burned down their houses and stole their food supplies. Eventually the natives laid siege to the Jamestown fort. Two out of every three colonists at James Fort starved to death.

Native Americans were also held in bondage, and there was a period when more indigenous people were exported into slavery through Charlestown than Africans were imported—but it never reached the level of the African slave trade.

★

From that moment when the first dark-skinned, half-naked, terrified, iron-shackled African person was marched off the ship and onto U.S. soil, and for the next 250 years, slavery would become an integral part of the nation and the engine of its economy.

From those original 20, the African slave population would explode—as colonists hungry to exploit the promised riches this new land offered, feasted on what seemed an inexhaustible source of free labor.

While exact numbers are impossible to determine, estimates are that 12.5 million Africans were sent to the "New World" between the seventeenth and nineteenth centuries. Of that number, some 10.6 million survived passage across the Atlantic.

Most slaves were sent to South America and the Caribbean Islands. Around 388,000 were shipped directly to America. Of course, at the start of the seventeenth century, the population of all the U.S. colonies was less than 500,000.

★

The term "plantation" arose as the southern settlements, originally linked with colonial expansion, came to revolve around the production of agriculture. Though wealthy aristocrats ruled the plantations, the laborers powered the system. The climate of the South was ideally suited to the cultivation of cash crops, like sugar, [usually in the form of rum made from molasses, a sugar byproduct] all over the world.

Planted on a large scale, sugar required a massive labor force. Sugar cane was a brutal crop. It demanded constant attention, every day. It maimed, burned, and killed those involved in its cultivation. The life span of an enslaved person on a sugar plantation could be as little as seven years.

The British poet William Cowper wrote, "I pity them greatly, but I must be mum, for how could we do without sugar or rum?" The sweetening of coffee and tea took precedence over human life and set the tone for slavery in the Americas.

★

In 1640, John Punch was a Black indentured servant of Virginia planter Hugh Gwyn, a wealthy landowner, justice, and member of the House of Burgesses, representing Charles River County. Punch ran away to Maryland accompanied by two of Gwyn's White European indentured—a Scotsman named James Gregory, and a Dutchman named Victor.

All three were quickly caught, returned, and tried before the Virginia Governor's Council, which served as the colony's highest court. The court sentenced both Europeans to have their terms of indenture extended by another four years. They sentenced Punch to "serve his said master or his assigns for the time of his natural life here or elsewhere."

All three men would also receive thirty lashes each.

★

Fifteen years after the Punch ruling, John Casor would become the first African to be legally declared a slave for life.

Anthony Johnson, one of the original "20 and odd negroes" aboard the *White Lion* was an indentured servant.

Indentured servitude allowed people who otherwise had no money for passage to work as a servant for free in exchange, and once having served for a specific period of time, earn their freedom.

After seven years, Johnson had served out his contract. As was common at the time, when a person completed his servitude, he was granted 50 acres of land. Johnson would go on to become a successful tobacco landowner and planter, employing five indentured servants of his own—Casor being one of them.

When Casor completed his seven years of service and asked for his freedom, Johnson initially refused but eventually allowed Casor to work for a White colonist named Robert Parker. A year later, Johnson changed his mind and brought suit against Parker for detaining his "Negro servant," saying "Hee never did see any [indenture] but that hee had ye Negro for his life."

In 1655, the court ruled in favor of Johnson, stating, "Mr. Robert Parker most unjustly keepeth the said Negro from Anthony Johnson his master ... It is therefore the Judgement of the Court and ordered That the said John Casor Negro forthwith returne unto the service of the said master Anthony Johnson, And that Mr. Robert Parker make payment of all charges in the suit."

Johnson, a free Black man, through the court decision, became the first slaveholder in the history of the United States.

In a cruel twist of the law, when Johnson died five years later, his 300 acres of land was passed to White colonists and not his children because the courts declared that as a Black man, Johnson was not a citizen of the colony.

★

Black slavery laws hardened in subsequent years. In 1662, the Virginia colony passed a law incorporating the principle of partus sequitur ventrem ("that which is brought forth follows the belly [womb]"), ruling that children of enslaved mothers would be born into slavery, regardless of their father's race or status.

In 1699, Virginia passed a law deporting all free Blacks.

Native American slavery and White indentured servitude were eventually phased out. White people were quickly prohibited from being slaves. In 1670, the colonial assembly passed a law prohibiting free and baptized Blacks and Indians from purchasing Christians, meaning Whites, but allowing them to buy people "of their owne nation."

The Virginia Slave Code of 1705 codified the status of slaves, establishing a set of rules based on the concept that enslaved persons were not persons at all; they were chattel—no better than a farm animal.

The code would also serve as a model for other colonies. It imposed harsh physical punishments on offending slaves, it required slaves to get written permission to leave their plantation; their testimony was inadmissible in any litigation involving Whites; they could make no contract, nor could they own property; even if attacked, they could not strike a White person; they could not assemble unless a White person was present; they could not own firearms; they could not be taught to read or write, nor could they transmit or possess "inflammatory" literature; and they were not permitted to marry.

★

One of the reasons slave codes were established was to prevent insurrections among slaves.

New York was originally under Dutch rule. Freed slaves had certain legal rights, such as the right to own land and to marry. After the English seized control, those rights went away.

New York City was not only a major hub for slave trade—with thousands of men, women and children passing through the slave market that operated in the heart of what is now the financial district—it had one of the largest slave populations of any of England's colonies.

Slaves worked as domestic servants, artisans, dock workers, and various skilled laborers. Many of the city's early landmarks, from City Hall to the eponymous wall of Wall Street were built using slave labor. Slaves also helped build the White House and the Capitol Building in Washington.

Slavery in New York differed from that of the South. There were no large planta-tions. In the densely populated city, slaves and free people often worked and lived in close proximity. Not only did that breed resentment among the city's slaves, but it was much easier for slaves to communicate with each other.

Things came to a head on the night of April 6, 1712, when a group of slaves took up arms and revolted against their captors. Twenty-three Black men, after gathering in an orchard, proceeded to set fire to the home of Peter Van Tilburgh on Maiden Lane near Broadway, at what was then the northern edge of Manhattan.

The fire was a signal to other slaves to begin the revolt. When the White colo-nists rushed out of their homes, they were confronted by a band of heavily-armed Blacks. The slaves fired into the crowd of Whites, causing panic.

Some Whites ran to the Battery (a fortification on the lower tip of Manhattan) to alert New York's governor, Robert Hunter, who sent the militia to deal with the rioters.

Hunter called it, "a bloody conspiracy of some of the slaves of this place, to destroy as many of the inhabitants as they could."

Upon seeing the soldiers the slaves ran north toward a wooded swamp and were eventually caught, many near present-day Canal Street.

Nine Whites were killed in the riot, six were wounded. Seventy Blacks were jailed. Twenty-seven were brought to trial, 21 were convicted and brutally executed: four were burned alive; one was crushed by a wheel; one was kept in chains until he starved to death; a pregnant woman was kept alive until she gave birth and was then executed; the others, quite benevolently, were just hanged. Six committed suicide rather than await trial.

"There has been the most exemplary punishment inflicted that could be possi-bly thought of," said Hunter.

Governor Hunter reimbursed the sheriff "thirty-six pounds and ten pence" for the cost of iron works, firewood and labor used in the executions (about $150,000 in modern currency).

In response to the slave rebellion, even stricter codes and punishments were enacted.

★

Slave rebellions were a continuous source of fear in the South, especially since Black slaves accounted for more than one-third of the region's population. It's estimated there were at least 250 slave rebellions in America before slavery was abolished in 1865.

The largest such uprising in Britain's North American colonies began in early September 1739 in South Carolina. Not long before, word had arrived that England and Spain were at war, raising hopes that the Spanish, who held Florida, would honor a proclamation stating that any slave who deserted to St. Augustine, Florida would be given their freedom.

The revolt's leader, Jemmy, was a literate Angolan slave. He started with 20 Congolese followers. The Blacks marched down the road with a banner that read "Liberty!" which they chanted in unison. They attacked a shop, killing the two store-keepers and seizing guns and gunpowder. Thus began the Stono Rebellion.

The rebels headed south toward St. Augustine and freedom. Along the road they gathered recruits, burned houses and killed Whites, sparing one innkeeper who was 'kind to his slaves.'" In all, they burned seven plantations and killed 25 Whites.

That afternoon, William Bull, South Carolina's lieutenant governor, and four companions, came across the rebels. They rode off to warn other slaveholders. Rallying a militia of planters, the colonists confronted them the following day.

In the ensuing battle, 20 Whites and 44 slaves were killed and the rebellion was largely contained. Some slaves who managed to escape were captured a week later. Most were executed, a few were sold to sugar planters in the West Indies.

★

In response to the rebellion, the South Carolina legislature passed the Negro Act of 1740. It restricted slave assembly, prohibited slaves from growing their own food, earning money, or learning to read.

It also enacted a 10-year moratorium against importing African slaves, encouraging a slave population who were native-born, believing them to be more "content" having grown up enslaved—rather than Africans, who were thought more rebellious.

Penalties were established against slaveholders' harsh treatment of slaves, but, these provisions were almost impossible to enforce since the law did not allow slave testimony against Whites.

★

The legislature tried to prevent slaves from being manumitted (being released from slavery), for fear that the presence of free Blacks in the colony made slaves restless. It required slaveholders to apply for permission for each case. South Carolina kept these restrictions until slavery was abolished after the Civil War.

There was another reason for the legislature's action: it reduced the chances that planters would set free the mixed-race children born of their families' "liaisons" (rape) with enslaved women, saving the planters from any public scrutiny or embarrassment that could arise.

The best-known example was the claim that Thomas Jefferson fathered as many as six children with Sally Hemings, an enslaved woman of mixed race, described as having "light skin, long straight hair and good looks."

Sally came to Jefferson's home as an infant as part of his wife Martha's inheritance of enslaved people from her father, John Wayles. She was the youngest of six children. At age 14, Sally accompanied Jefferson's younger daughter Mary "Polly" to London and then to Paris, where the widowed Jefferson, aged 44 at the time, was serving as the United States Minister to France.

Hemings spent two years there, before returning to Monticello with the family. Upon Jefferson's death, Hemings was "given her time" by his daughter in an informal freedom. She lived her last nine years as a free woman.

When confronted over the allegations that Hemings was his "concubine" and had born him children, Jefferson always refused to speak about it. A 1998 DNA study found a match between the Jefferson male line and a descendant of Hemings' last son.

★

In the early 1800s, a series of revivals swept across the colonies to convert slaves to Christianity.

Leading the crusade was George Whitefield, an English revivalist. He considered it the duty of slave owners to bring their slaves to Christ. Whitefield stressed that slave converts would owe absolute obedience to their owners, just as they did to God.

Some slave owners embraced the idea. There were those masters, however, that didn't allow their slaves to go to church, ridiculing the notion of religion for slaves because they refused to believe that Black people had souls.

As one slave explained, "White folks 'fraid the N*****s git to thinkin' they was free, if they had churches 'n things."

Slaves frequently were moved to hold their own religious meetings out of disgust for the depraved gospel expounded by their master's preachers.

★

Slaves often faced severe punishment if caught attending secret prayer meetings. Author, abolitionist, and, for more than the first four decades of his life, an enslaved person, Moses Grandy, reported that his brother-in-law Isaac, a slave preacher, "was flogged, and his back pickled" for preaching at a clandestine service in the woods. His listeners were also flogged and "forced to tell who else was there."

Besides the obvious punishment of just being a slave, corporal punishment was a routine part of life as a slave. Slaves found guilty of murder or rape would be hanged. For minor offenses, such as associating with Whites, slaves would be whipped, branded, or maimed. For more serious offenses, slaves would receive sixty lashes and be placed in stocks, where his or her ears would be cut off.

Methodist minister Charles Wesley was shocked to overhear talk among slave owners about meting out punishment. A "gentleman" recommended that one "first nail up a negro by the ears, then order him to be whipped in the severest manner, and then to have scalding water thrown over him, so that the poor creature could not stir for four months after."

In Louisiana, a free Black convicted of torturing and killing a White girl was sentenced to have her right hand cut off before being hanged. The court ordered that after her death her head should be "stuck up upon a pole at her former place of residence" with her "hand to be nailed to the same post."

★

American colonists had more to worry about than keeping their slaves in line. Trouble had been brewing for some time with their English masters. Britain, in an effort to fund its war debt and the cost of it ever-expanding British Empire, decided to establish new levies on its American counterparts.

In 1765, Parliament passed the Stamp Act as one such revenue measure. Colonists condemned the tax because their rights as Englishmen protected them from any tax in which they had no elected Parliamentary representatives.

"Taxation without representation." It was cruel and unusual punishment.

★

On the evening of March 5, 1770, British troops fired into a crowd of angry American colonists in Boston who had taunted and violently harassed them. Five colonists were killed. The event, which became known as the Boston Massacre, helped fuel the outrage against British rule and spurred on the Revolution.

Among those killed was a rope-maker of mixed Black and American Indian descent named Crispus Attucks.

His father was an enslaved African and his mother was a Native woman who was a member of the Wampanoag tribe. Attucks spent most of his youth enslaved by a man named William Browne. At age 27, he ran away.

In a newspaper advertisement published in 1750, Browne announced the escape of a "Molatto fellow" named Crispus, and described him as 6'2" with short, curly hair, wearing a bearskin coat, buckskin breeches and a checked shirt when he fled. He was apparently knock-kneed, too.

Attucks made his way to Boston, where he became a sailor, one of the few trades open to a non-White person.

On the evening of the massacre, Attucks was outside a pub when he and other patrons confronted some British soldiers. Since he had escaped slavery, his defiance took considerable courage—given he faced the risk of being arrested and returned to servitude.

A witness described Attucks, "this stout man," stepping into the fray and swinging his stick at Captain Thomas Preston, and then knocking away a soldier's gun and hitting him in the face or head. Attucks then grabbed the soldier's bayonet in his other hand and then yelled for the crowd to "kill the dogs, knock them over," just moments before the soldier regained control of his gun and shot him.

He was struck twice in the chest by two musket balls, one which tore an inch-wide hole in his chest, inflicting a lethal injury. The jury acquitted the soldiers of murder in the deaths of Attucks and four colonists killed in the brawl (though two were convicted of the lesser crime of manslaughter and branded on their hands as a punishment and then released).

In death, Attucks was afforded honors that no person of color, particularly one who had escaped slavery, probably had ever received before in America.

Samuel Adams organized a procession to transport Attucks' casket to Boston's Faneuil Hall, where it lay in state for three days before the victims' public funeral attended by an estimated 10,000 to 12,000

★

The American Revolution occurred between 1775 and 1783. The American Patriots in the Thirteen Colonies ultimately defeated the British, winning independence and establishing the United States of America. But it would be a long, hard-fought battle.

On the eve of the American Revolution, slaves constituted a large portion of the colony's population. For instance, in the tobacco-producing regions of the Chesapeake, more than half the inhabitants were slaves—ironic that a nation that had become a slave society bristled at being slaves to a foreign nation.

Skirmishes between British troops and colonial militiamen in Lexington and Concord in April 1775 kicked off the armed conflict, and by the following summer, the rebels were waging a full-scale war for their independence.

General George Washington, revising an earlier edict (having previously decreed that "neither negroes, boys unable to bear arms, nor old men" could enlist in the Continental Army), ordered recruiting officers to accept free Blacks in the American Army. More than 5,000, mostly Black Northerners, fought against the British.

The British, in turn, promised protection and freedom to all slaves in the colonies who escaped from their patriot masters. Some 20,000 Black slaves joined the British during the American Revolution.

France entered the American Revolution on the side of the colonists in 1778, turning what had essentially been a civil war into an international conflict. After French assistance helped the Continental Army force the British surrender at Yorktown, Virginia in 1781, the Americans had effectively won their independence, though fighting would not formally end until 1783.

The subsequent peace negotiations called for all slaves who escaped behind British lines before November 30, 1782, to be freed with restitution given to their owners. With their certificates of freedom in hand, 3,000 Black men, women, and children joined the Loyalist exodus from New York to Nova Scotia in 1783. There they found freedom, but little else.

After years of economic hardship and denial of the land and provisions they had been promised, nearly half abandoned the Canadian province. Approximately 400 sailed to London, while in 1792 more than 1,200 brought their stories full circle and returned to Africa in a new settlement in Sierra Leone.

Among the newly relocated was the former slave of the newly elected president of the United States, Harry Washington, who returned to the land of his birth.

★

As famously written into the Declaration of Independence, a newly-freed America was founded on the principle that "We hold these truths to be self-evident that all men are created equal, that they are endowed by their Creator with certain unalienable Rights, that among these are Life, Liberty and the pursuit of Happiness."

Somehow slaves were good enough to fight against the British, but they weren't good enough to gain their liberty. That became a moral dilemma for many in the North. Over the next three decades every Northern state would abolish slavery.

It was a different case in the South. Americans had finally gained the right to control their lives and their property, which included other human beings.

Ten years after the war ended, the United States Congress passed the Fugitive Slave Clause, "an Act respecting fugitives from justice, and persons escaping from the service of their masters."

The measure met with strong opposition in the Northern states, some of which enacted personal liberty laws to hamper the execution of the federal law (providing that fugitives who appealed an original decision against them were entitled to a jury trial), but in the end, was passed by a vote of 48–7, with 14 abstaining.

Simply stated, this law put fugitive slaves at risk for recapture the rest of their lives. One famous case involved Oney Judge, one of Martha Washington's slaves.

George Washington, "Father of His Country," who played a key role in adopting and ratifying the Constitution, was then elected president (twice), who was appointed Commanding General of the Continental Army and was instrumental in America gaining her freedom from England, owned slaves—as did most founding fathers, such as Thomas Jefferson, John Jay, James Madison, and Benjamin Franklin.

Oney helped dress her mistress, frequently accompanying her on shopping trips, and traveled with the Washingtons between their homes in Philadelphia and Washington (at the time, Philadelphia was America's capital). To evade the abolition law that took effect in Pennsylvania in 1780, the Washingtons made sure to transport their enslaved workers in and out of the state every six months to avoid them establishing legal residency.

In the spring of 1796, Oney learned that Martha Washington planned to give her away as a wedding gift to her granddaughter, Elizabeth Parke Custis. Twenty-two-year-old Oney slipped away one night while the Washingtons were having dinner out. Oney was hidden by friends until she could find passage on a northbound ship, eventually ending up in Portsmouth, New Hampshire.

Mrs. Washington felt betrayed and claimed that Oney must have been abducted and seduced by a Frenchman. She urged the President to advertise a reward for Oney's recapture, but Washington refused, realizing how unpopular that would be.

Later that summer, a friend of the Washington's spotted Oney walking on a street in Portsmouth. Washington asked Secretary of the Treasury Oliver Wolcott to handle the matter, who wrote to Joseph Whipple, the Collector of Customs of Portsmouth, requesting his help in the return of the President's wife's property. Nothing came of it.

Several attempts were made to convince Oney to return, and when those failed, a kidnapping plot was hatched. However, word got to her and she went into hiding.

While Washington's feelings about slavery had changed over the years, as he expressed his uneasiness with the institution to close friends, it was a different matter when it came to relinquishing the bound labor on which his Virginia plantation—and his life—was built. He wanted his property back.

When Washington died in 1799, he did insert a provision in his will freeing all 67 of his enslaved workers upon his wife's death. Martha Washington, on the other hand, who lived until 1802, never emancipated her 150 enslaved workers upon her death.

Oney Judge would spend the rest of her life as a fugitive.

★

Mum Bett, on the other hand, was able to win her freedom.

In 1780, in the midst of America's war for independence, "all men are born free and equal," rang out from the central square in the small town of Sheffield in western Massachusetts. The inspiring line was from the state's newly ratified constitution, read aloud for a proud public to hear.

But one woman who heard it wasn't inspired. She was enraged. Elizabeth Freeman, then known only as "Bett," was an enslaved woman to the household of Colonel John Ashley. As she watched the men around her declare freedom from oppressive rule, it only stood to reason that she should do the same.

"I heard that paper read yesterday, that says all men are born equal and that every man has a right to freedom," she said, "I am not a dumb critter; won't the law give me my freedom?"

Freeman marched to the house of Theodore Sedgwick, a prominent local lawyer. He agreed to take the case, which was joined by another of Ashley's slaves, a man called Brom.

Brom & Bett v. Ashley was argued before a county court. The jury ruled in favor of Bett and Brom, making them the first enslaved Blacks to be freed under the Massachusetts Constitution of 1780, and ordered Ashley to pay them thirty shillings and costs.

Elizabeth Freeman died in 1829 at the age of 85, a free woman, surrounded by her children and grandchildren in the Free State of Massachusetts that she had helped to create.

★

For most slaves, ownership was impossible. That even included their name, which was usually decided by their owner.

Many newborns were given Anglicized names, like Jack, Thomas, Hannah or Elizabeth. Biblical names were common, like "Moses," as were names like "January" or "Easter," which usually indicated when the child was born. "Sambo" was usually meant to indicate a second child. Pet names were popular, like "Caesar" or "Venus." To show contempt, captors would name a child "Buck" or "Wench," or simply "Boy" or "Gal."

To maintain some form of dignity, many slaves had two names: the one given by the slave owner, such as "Brutus," and a private name, like "Sabe," "Bumbo," "Taynay," or "Yearie," used in the slave quarters.

★

In 1792, recent college graduate Eli Whitney moved to Georgia to work as a tutor on a plantation of Catherine Greene, the widow of American Revolutionary War hero, General Nathanael Greene.

At the time, cotton was not a profitable crop—due to all the manual labor needed to remove the seeds from cotton plants. With Eli Whitney's patenting of a cotton gin (at the time, Blacks were not permitted to file a patent. Whitney stole the idea from a slave known only by the name Sam), cotton lint could be produced fast and efficiently at up to 50 pounds per day.

Cotton quickly became America's leading export. For the North, especially New England, cotton's rise meant a steady supply of raw materials for its textile mills. The cotton gin had transformed the American economy.

Much to abolitionists' chagrin, over the next two decades the slave population would double, with emphasis on the breeding of slaves for a revitalized slave market. Families were often split up, as children were born specifically to be a marketable product and ended up being sold to other plantations to meet the increased need.

At the time, there were some 790,000 slaves. Two decades later, the slave population would approach 1.2 million.

★

In the spring of 1800, inspired in part by the American colonists' revolt against Britain and by the success of a slave revolt in the French colony of St. Domingue (Haiti) in 1791, a group of slaves in Virginia plotted to seize the city of Richmond.

Sam Byrd Jr., a slave of widow Jane Clarke, had joined with George Smith, an enslaved man of another widow, Ann Smith. Also in on the plot was Jack Bowler, who was owned by a widow in Caroline County. And there was Gabriel, a blacksmith owned by Thomas Henry Prosser, who emerged as the most significant leader of the scheme.

The plotters in Gabriel's Conspiracy, as it came to be known, regularly met in the shade of bridges, near springs, at religious gatherings, and after a funeral. By August, a plan had been devised that included a nighttime attack on Richmond.

The blacksmiths refashioned scythe blades into swords; one witness claimed that twelve dozen such weapons were created. Jack Bowler reported that he had made fifty pikes, or spears, by affixing bayonets to the ends of poles. Bowler, Gabriel, and another plotter amassed stores of gunpowder, and Gabriel and his brother, Martin, made musket balls for the cache of firearms they planned to seize.

The rendezvous scheduled for the night of August 30 never took place. Two slaves betrayed the others just hours before a torrential rainstorm prevented the "conspirators" from gathering (unaware of the betrayal, the leaders postponed the attack for one night). By then, patrols had already begun detaining suspects—the revolt collapsed. Gabriel and Jack Bowler, the two most senior men in charge, disappeared.

Virginia authorities arrested and prosecuted more than 70 enslaved men for insurrection and conspiracy. Once the first ten men had been hanged, Governor James Monroe, a Founding Father who would go on to become the fifth president of the United States, asked Thomas Jefferson how many executions might be necessary to prevent another uprising.

Five days later, by which time another five men had been executed, Jefferson responded that his neighbors thought there had been enough. Monroe proposed to his council that condemned men be reprieved until the next meeting of the assembly, but the council refused.

Still, as more men were sentenced to death, the expense of reimbursing owners for the loss of their slaves grew uncomfortably steep, and executive pardons began to replace trips to the gallows. In the end, it wasn't about justice or mercy. It was about money.

The two men who revealed the plot, were rewarded with their freedom after the General Assembly authorized their purchase and manumission.

The aborted uprising also provoked refinements in the state's slave laws at the next meeting of the General Assembly, including the adoption of transportation as an alternative to capital punishment for some slave offenders and calls for an end to private manumissions and for the deportation of free Blacks.

★

Over the years, many northern states enacted legislation to protect free Black Americans (who could otherwise be abducted, brought before court without the ability to produce a defense, and then lawfully enslaved) as well as runaway slaves. Those laws came to be known as personal liberty laws and required slave owners and fugitive hunters to produce evidence that their captures were truly fugitive slaves.

A prominent example was Solomon Northup, born free around 1808 to Mintus Northup and his wife in Essex County, New York. Northup was tricked into going to Washington, DC, where slavery was legal. He was drugged, kidnapped, and sold into bondage, and he was held as a slave in Louisiana for 12 years.

One of the very few to regain freedom under such circumstances, he later sued the slave traders involved. Washington, DC. Law prohibited Northrup from testifying against the White men. He lost the case.

★

In 1807, Congress implemented the Act Prohibiting Importation of Slaves, which became effective on January 1st of the following year. It terminated the country's involvement in the international slave trade. The Slave Trade Act of 1794 had ended the legality of American ships participating in the trade. This bill served to prohibit any importation of slaves into the country and made it a federal crime.

It did nothing to stop slavery. The slave population continued to grow.

The Three-Fifths Clause that the planter elite had secured in the Constitution only served to reinforce the brutal system of slavery—because three-fifths of the enslaved population was counted in determining a state's population and thus its congressional representation.

President Thomas Jefferson wrote in his 1808 State of the Union address, "I congratulate you, fellow-citizens, on the approach of the period at which you may interpose [use] your authority constitutionally to withdraw the citizens of the United States from all further participation in those violations of human rights which have been so long continued on the unoffending inhabitants of Africa."

Of course, like Washington, Jefferson's public pronouncements about human rights were a far cry from the conflict he had over his dependence on slave labor to run his many businesses. For instance, a year before the speech, Jefferson was at Monticello, when Edmund Bacon, overseer of his estate advised him that one of the slaves had stolen a large hoard of nails (Jefferson had a nailery on his property) and that he was certain that James Hubbard, one of the slaves, was responsible,

Only a few years before, in the summer of 1805, Hubbard had vanished. Several weeks later Jefferson received a letter from the sheriff of Fairfax County. Hubbard was in custody. He had confessed to being an escaped slave.

Hubbard was returned to Monticello. There is no record of any punishment. In fact, it seems that Hubbard was forgiven and regained Jefferson's trust. An 1806 schedule shows Hubbard's daily output of 15 pounds of nails. That Christmas, Jefferson allowed him to travel from Monticello to Poplar Forest to see his family.

When the theft was brought to light, Jefferson was "very much surprised and felt very badly about it," because Hubbard "had always been a favorite servant." Jefferson said he would question Hubbard personally the next morning when he went on his usual ride past Bacon's house.

When Jefferson showed up the next day Hubbard burst into tears, begging Jefferson's pardon "over and over again." For a slave, burglary was a capital crime. A runaway slave who once broke into Bacon's private storehouse and stole three pieces of bacon and a bag of cornmeal was condemned to hang in Albemarle County. The governor commuted his sentence, and the slave was "transported," the legal term for being sold by the state to the Deep South or West Indies.

Instead of being hanged or whipped, though, Jefferson turned to Bacon and said, "Ah, sir, we can't punish him. He has suffered enough already." Hubbard seemed repentant, asking permission to go and be baptized---but it was a ruse to escape. He made his way to the town of Lexington, where he was able to live for over a year as a free man, being in possession of an impeccable (forged) manumission document.

His description appeared in the Richmond Enquirer: "a Nailor by trade, of 27 years of age, about six feet high, stout limbs and strong made, of daring demeanor, bold and harsh features, dark complexion, apt to drink freely and had even furnished himself with money and probably a free pass; on a former elopement he attempted to get out of the State Northwardly ... and probably may have taken the same direction now."

Jefferson would eventually put a slave tracker on his trail. Cornered and clapped in irons, Hubbard was brought back to Monticello, where Jefferson "had him severely flogged in the presence of his old companions and committed to jail." Jefferson sold Hubbard to one of his overseers. His final fate is not known.

Jefferson wasn't able to understand how someone he placed so much faith and trust in would want to turn on him like that.

★

The plot organized by Denmark Vesey, a free Black carpenter from Charleston, North Carolina—who had purchased his freedom in December 1799 with lottery winnings—was perhaps the largest and most audacious slave uprising in North American history.

Vesey had joined the city's new African Methodist Episcopal congregation. It quickly became the center of Charleston's enslaved community. The temporary closure of the church by city authorities in June 1818, and the arrest of 140 congregants, only reinforced the determination of Vessey and others to maintain a place of independent worship and established the motivation for his conspiracy.

Vesey decided to orchestrate a rebellion followed by a mass exodus from Charleston to Haiti. President Jean-Pierre Boyer had recently encouraged Black Americans to bring their skills and capital to his beleaguered island republic.

For four long years, Vesey planned the escape. It is said that thousands of slaves were prepared to join in. The plan called for Vesey's followers to rise at midnight on Sunday, 14 July—Bastille Day—slay their masters, and sail for Haiti and freedom. He encouraged his followers to arm themselves with swords or long daggers, which in any case would make for quieter work as the city bells tolled at midnight.

The plot unraveled in June 1822 when two slaves revealed the plan to their owners. Mayor James Hamilton called up the city militia and convened a special court to try the captured insurgents.

Vesey was captured, along with five other rebels, the men collectively "met their fate with the heroic fortitude of Martyrs." In all, thirty-five slaves were executed. Forty-two others were sold as slaves in Spanish Cuba.

In the aftermath, Charleston authorities demolished the African Church. The state assembly subsequently passed laws prohibiting the entry of free Blacks into the state, and city officials enforced ordinances against teaching Blacks to read.

★

By the beginning of the next decade, in 1830, the slave population in America had topped two million.

In late January, Daniel Webster, Senator from Massachusetts, rose in the Senate to proclaim, "Liberty and Union, now and forever, one and inseparable!" Some historians regard Webster's oration, which stretched over two days, as the most famous speech ever to be delivered in Senate annals. It established him as a national figure who would lead the debate over the nature of the Union for two more tumultuous decades.

Webster spoke in response to Senator Robert Hayne in a debate that initially focused on efforts to limit federal land sales in the West but soon shifted to the larger issue of slavery and the proper role of the federal government.

Speaking to a packed chamber, Webster, who had entered the Senate two years earlier, held that the nation was not an association of sovereign states, from which individual states could withdraw at will, but rather a "popular government, erected by the people; those who administer it are responsible to the people; and itself capable of being amended and modified, just as the people may choose it should be."

Following his speech, Webster encountered Hayne at a White House reception. When Webster asked him how he was doing, Hayne replied, "None the better for you, sir."

★

Denmark Vesey may have planned the largest slave revolt, but it was Nathanial "Nat" Turner who, in 1831, would lead the bloodiest.

Spreading dread throughout the White South, his reign of terror—what today would be called his fight for freedom—still hangs over the sandy soil and blackwater cypress swamps of North Carolina, even if physical traces of the event may have vanished.

At noon on August 21, six slaves met in the secluded swampy woodlands around Cabin Pond, in a neighborhood known as "The Cross Keys." They ate, spoke, and enjoyed a roasted pig. At three o'clock, a seventh man joined them. It was Nat Turner. He was short, stout, but powerfully built, with a dark "mulatto" complexion.

Turner was born on the Virginia plantation of Benjamin Turner. During a period when most Blacks were not educated, his master's son instructed him in reading, writing, and religion.

His wisdom and natural orating skills led Nat to become a fiery preacher, claiming that he was chosen by God to lead them from bondage. Other slaves called him "the Prophet." Hearing divine voices, Turner was convinced that the time to rise up had come. This religious framework was of central importance to him, a manifestation of the Biblical injunction, "an eye for an eye, a tooth for a tooth."

As a hush came over the assembled group, a vow was made: to kill all slave owners they encounter, including women and children. They decided the first victims would be Turner's current master, Joseph Travis.

The conspirators waited until midnight. Turner entered the home through an open second-story window, then crept downstairs and let the others in. The rebels hacked the sleeping Travis and his wife to pieces. An infant sleeping nearby in a crib was decapitated, its body then cast into the fireplace; two young boys—about three and seven years of age—were likewise beheaded, along with an orphaned sixteen-year-old apprentice who had the misfortune to be staying with the family.

"Each child's bed a crimson, wooden tomb," noted a journalist.

Some of the enslaved chose not to join the revolt. Some even fought to protect their masters—but a considerable number did join the group—first fifteen, then forty, then sixty—some armed with muskets, some with axes, some with knives; some came on their masters' horses; they split up, and the appalling work was carried on more rapidly still.

"Whole families, father, mother, daughters, sons, sucking babes, and school children" were "butchered, thrown into heaps, and left to be devoured by hogs and dogs, or to putrefy on the spot."

The revolt lasted two days, during which fifty-five Whites were slain. Many were women and children.

By this point Turner's band had dwindled to about 20. It found itself beset by armed state militia. The group dissolved as some were killed or captured, and some, including Turner, ran away.

The short-lived insurrection over, vengeance began. Men were tortured to death, burned, maimed, and subjected to nameless atrocities. Some 200 Black people would die.

"They killed Antonio, a slave of Mr. J. Stanley, whom they shot; then they pointed their guns at him and told him to confess about the insurrection. He told 'em he didn't know anything about any insurrection. They shot several balls through him, quartered him, and put his head on a pole at the fork of the road leading to the court."

"A party of horsemen started from Richmond with the intention of killing every colored person they saw in Southampton County. They stopped opposite the cabin of a free-colored man, who was hoeing in his little field. They called out, 'Is this Southampton County?' He replied, 'Yes, Sir, you have just crossed the line, by yonder tree.' They shot him dead and rode on."

Turner managed to elude capture for two months, hiding out in a crude cave he fashioned—a hole dug under a pile of wood—before surrendering. He was tried a few days later for "conspiring to rebel and making insurrection." He was convicted and sentenced to death, hanged and his corpse was drawn and quartered.

More than 50 slaves were eventually brought to trial. Eighteen were executed, 12 were transported and sold South, and 21 were discharged to return to their masters. Of those executed, at least seven slaveowners sent legislative petitions for compensation for the loss of their slaves without trials during or immediately after the insurrection. They were all rejected.

★

Margaret Morgan was born in the shadow of freedom. Her parents were slaves of John Ashmore, a prosperous Maryland mill owner who, while he freed many of his slaves in the last years of his life, never laid claim to Margaret.

Margaret married Jerry Morgan, a free Black man, took his last name, moved to the free state of Pennsylvania, and started a family. A few years later, in 1837, Ashmore's widow sent Edward Prigg, an attorney, justice of the peace, and part-time slave catcher (along with three companions), to retrieve her "property."

Somehow, although he had no title of ownership, Prigg obtained a warrant to reclaim Margaret. The whole family was seized in the middle of the night and forced "into an open wagon in a cold sleety rain." The captors released Jerry Morgan, assuring him they would settle the issue in the morning.

As soon as Jerry was out of sight, the slave catchers took Margaret and her children across the state line into Maryland, where the family was immediately sold to a slave trader to be transported to the south.

The kidnapping touched off an interstate court battle that involved the governors of both states. Jerry Morgan fought to have his wife freed, making several trips to the Pennsylvania state capital to petition the governor. It would cost him his life, because, on one such journey, Morgan drowned after jumping overboard from a Susquehanna River ferry after a group of White passengers and crew accused him of stealing a coat.

Prigg and his group were charged with kidnapping in Pennsylvania and convicted in 1839. They appealed and the case eventually found its way to the Supreme Court, which in 1842 voided the conviction by ruling Pennsylvania's law violated both the Constitution's Article IV, which allowed the return of persons escaping from one state to another, and the Fugitive Slave Act of 1793. The federal law, said the court, superseded the state's.

The Prigg case had far-reaching significance in stirring the sectional (loyalty to one's own region, rather than to the country as a whole) controversy over slavery. Since the Supreme Court supported the side of slaveholders, free states were crippled in their ability to maintain rule of law as slave catchers grew bolder—and more prosperous.

Increasing refusal of abolitionists in the free states to comply with the 1793 law and the ruling in Prigg prompted southern representatives to demand a stricter Fugitive Slave Act in the Compromise of 1850.

★

While the United States had abolished the importation of slaves, slavery itself remained legal in most parts of the world. Along the coast of present-day Sierra Leone, for example, a notorious Spanish slave trader Pedro Blanco is said to have lived partly like a European aristocrat and partly like an African king—having built himself a private nation-state with storehouses on an island, his office on another island, and houses for his African wives on yet a third island.

Blanco controlled a slave trading network that fed Cuba's insatiable hunger for plantation workers. He would conduct over fifty voyages to West Indies island.

In February and March of 1839, fifty-three Africans who would later find themselves on the *Amistad,* arrived at Blanco's slave depot, known as Lomboko, after being force-marched there from Sierra Leone's interior. Most had been kidnapped, some captured in warfare, or taken as debt repayment, or prisoners punished for such crimes as adultery.

Kept in a slave barracks, disease, famine and beatings were commonplace. After several weeks in captivity, they and 500 or so other captives were loaded onto the slave ship *Tecora.*

According to testimony that the *Amistad* captives later gave, they were shackled around the ankles, wrists, and neck and forced to sleep tightly together in contorted positions, with not enough headroom to even stand up straight.

Following two months at sea, the *Tecora* landed in Havana, Cuba, where 49 adults and 4 children were purchased for $450 each, with plans to bring them to sugar plantations a few hundred miles away in Puerto Príncipe (now Camagüey), Cuba.

The slaves were loaded onto the *Amistad* and, under the cover of nightfall so as to best avoid British antislavery patrols, departed from Havana. The ship also carried a cargo of dishes, cloth, jewelry, and various luxury items and staples. The cargo was insured for $40,000. The adult slaves were insured for $20,000 and the children for $1,300.

The captives continued suffering severe mistreatment, so one night they agreed to band together in revolt. Led by Cinqué, a rice farmer, in the early morning of July 2, using a loose spike removed from the deck, they picked the locks on their chains, climbed up to the main deck and bludgeoned the cook to death.

Awakened by the ruckus, the crew grabbed anything in reach to defend themselves, The captain managed to kill one African and mortally wound another—but he was eventually slashed to death with cane knives the captives had found in the ship's hold. The crew was ordered to sail back to Sierra Leone.

Having all grown up away from the ocean, the Africans depended on the crew for navigation. During the day, the Spaniards set an eastward course, as they had been told to do. At night, however, they sailed westward, hoping to remain in Cuban waters, but a gale drove the ship northeast along the United States coastline. With little to drink onboard, dehydration and dysentery took a toll, and several Africans ended up dying.

News soon got around about a mysterious ship in the neighborhood with her "sails nearly all blown to pieces." Some reports said that Cuban slaves had revolted and killed the crew of a Spanish ship and were roaming the Atlantic as buccaneers.

On August 26, a U.S. Navy brig ran into the *Amistad* off the eastern end of Long Island. The crew was freed, while the Africans were imprisoned.

Thousands of curious visitors paid the jailers an admission fee to come look at these creatures. Media coverage was extensive, and by September 2, a New York City theater was already putting on a play entitled "The Long, Low Black Schooner."

Prosecutors argued that, as slaves, the mutineers were subject to the laws governing conduct between slaves and their masters. But trial testimony determined that while slavery was legal in Cuba, importation of slaves from Africa was not. Therefore, the judge ruled, rather than being merchandise, the Africans were victims of kidnapping and had the right to escape their captors in any way they could.

When the U.S. government appealed the case before the Supreme Court the next year, congressman and former president John Quincy Adams argued eloquently for the *Amistad* rebels. The higher court upheld the lower court, and private and missionary society donations helped the surviving Africans secure passage home.

★

Empathizing with the plight of slaves was not an easy concept for many Americans. Two books would change that.

Frederick Douglass's brilliant prose and soaring oratory pricked the conscience of a nation. Through his autobiographies, Douglass told his extraordinary personal story. He poignantly described the young slave who mastered the master's language, and who saw to the core of the meaning of slavery, both for individuals and for the nation. And then he captured the multiple meanings of freedom—as idea and reality, of mind and body—as no one else ever did in America.

Douglass's first of a three-volume, 1,200-page series, *Narrative of the Life of Frederick Douglass, An American Slave,* was published in 1845.

Frederick Augustus Washington Bailey was born around 1818 into slavery. Defying a ban on teaching slaves to read and write, his Baltimore slaveholder Hugh Auld's wife, Sophia, taught Douglass the alphabet when he was around 12.

It was through reading that Douglass' ideological opposition to slavery began to take shape. He read newspapers avidly and sought out political writing and literature as much as possible.

Douglass was later made to work for Edward Covey, who had a reputation as a "slave-breaker." Covey's constant abuse nearly broke the 16-year-old Douglass psychologically. Eventually, however, Douglass fought back, in a scene rendered powerfully in his first autobiography. Douglass tried to escape from slavery twice before he finally succeeded—thanks to Anna Murray, a free Black woman he would later marry.

Douglass was eventually asked to tell his story at abolitionist meetings, and he became a regular anti-slavery lecturer. As his fame grew, fearing recapture, he spent two years overseas. During this time, his supporters gathered funds to purchase his freedom.

After his return, Douglass would spend almost a half century more bettering the lives of Blacks. In 1877, Douglass met with Thomas Auld, the man who once owned him, and the two reportedly reconciled.

In 1882, after his first wife's death, Douglass married Helen Pitts, a feminist from Honeoye, New York. Their marriage caused quite a stir, since Pitts was White and nearly 20 years younger than Douglass.

Douglass remained active until his death in 1895. He died after suffering a heart attack on his way home from a meeting of the National Council of Women, a feminist rights group still in its infancy at the time.

★

The book that would have a most profound impact on the American public on the issue of slavery, was *Uncle Tom's Cabin*. The story goes that when President Abraham Lincoln met the author, Harriet Beecher Stowe, at the start of the Civil War he stated, "so this is the little lady who made this big war."

Published in 1852, *Uncle Tom's Cabin* tells the story of Uncle Tom, depicted as a saintly, dignified slave. While being transported by boat to auction in New Orleans, Tom saves the life of Little Eva, whose grateful father then purchases Tom. Eva and Tom soon become great friends. Always frail, Eva's health begins to decline rapidly, and on her deathbed she asks her father to free all his slaves. He makes plans to do so but is then killed, and the brutal Simon Legree, Tom's new owner, has Tom whipped to death after he refuses to divulge the whereabouts of certain runaway slaves.

Tom maintains a steadfastly Christian attitude toward his own suffering, and Stowe imbues Tom's death with echoes of Christ's (a big reason why the story appealed to a White audience).

Uncle Tom's Cabin was the most popular nineteenth-century novel and, after the *Bible*, was the second-best-selling book of that century. Over 300,000 copies were sold in the United States in its first year alone.

Through the pages, readers became acutely aware of the horrors of slavery on a far more personal level than ever before. In the South, not too surprisingly, the book was met with outrage and branded an irresponsible product of distortions and overstatements. It only served to further divide the nation's moral conscious.

★

When it came to the law, however, there was no question where the government stood. In 1857, Dred Scott, who was enslaved, went to court to claim his freedom after his enslaver transported him into a free state and territory. The Supreme Court determined his fate when Chief Justice Roger B. Taney stated that Blacks are "so far inferior that they had no rights which the white man was bound to respect, and that the negro might justly and lawfully be reduced to slavery for his benefit."

By statute and interpretation of the law, Black people in America were dehumanized and commodified in order to maintain the economic and political power supported by slavery.

★

A few years after Frederick Douglass's autobiography was released and just before *Uncle Tom's Cabin* came out, Harriet Tubman would escape her bondage—then conduct over a dozen missions to rescue approximately 70 enslaved people using the network of antislavery activists and safe houses known as the Underground Railroad.

Born a slave in Dorchester County, Maryland, as a child Tubman was beaten and whipped by her various masters. She would suffer a severe head wound when an irate slave owner threw a heavy metal weight intending to hit another slave, but struck her instead. Besides the physical trauma, Tubman began experiencing strange visions and vivid dreams, which she ascribed to premonitions from God. These experiences, combined with her Methodist upbringing, led her to become devoutly religious.

Tubman escaped to Philadelphia in 1849, only to return to rescue her family. Slowly, one group at a time, she brought relatives with her out of the state, and eventually guided dozens of other slaves to freedom.

Traveling by night and in extreme secrecy, Tubman (or "Moses", as she was called) "never lost a passenger."

When the Civil War began, Tubman worked for the Union Army, first as a cook and nurse, and then as an armed scout and spy. The first woman to lead an armed expedition in the war, she guided the raid at Combahee Ferry, which liberated more than 700 slaves.

After the war, she was active in the women's suffrage movement until illness overtook her, and she had to be admitted to a home for elderly Blacks that she had helped to establish years earlier in 1908. Harriet Tubman died in 1913 at the age of 93.

★

Prior to becoming a staunch abolitionist who advocated the use of armed insurrection to overthrow the institution of slavery in the United States, John Brown ran tannery and cattle trading businesses, until the brutal murder of Presbyterian minister and anti-slavery activist Elijah P. Lovejoy in 1837.

"Here, before God, in the presence of these witnesses," Brown exclaimed, "from this time, I consecrate my life to the destruction of slavery!"

Brown first gained national attention when he led small groups of volunteers during the Bleeding Kansas crisis of 1856—a series of violent civil confrontations which emerged from a political and ideological debate over the legality of slavery in the proposed state of Kansas.

Tempers flared to such a fevered pitch over the issue that, after addressing "the crime against Kansas," Senator Charles Sumner from Massachusetts was attacked with a cane and beaten unconscious on the Senate floor.

By early 1859, Brown was leading raids to free slaves in areas where forced labor was still in practice, primarily in the present-day Midwest. Brown began planning an attack on slaveholders, as well as a United States military armory at Harpers Ferry, Virginia (now West Virginia).

He planned to use armed freed slaves, and hoped the attack would help lay the groundwork for a slave revolt. In some respects he was right. Historians have called the raid a dress rehearsal for the Civil War.

Brown recruited 22 men in all, including his sons Owen and Watson, and several freed slaves. The operation began on October 16, 1859. Its success depended on the seizure of the fort's armory before officials in Washington, D.C. were made aware and could send in reinforcements.

John Brown's men had stopped a Baltimore & Ohio Railroad train headed for the nation's capital, but, unfortunately chose to let the train continue. The conductor notified authorities about the pending raid.

To make matters worse, the first casualty of the raid was a baggage handler at the town's train station, who was shot in the back and killed when he refused the orders of Brown's men. The victim was a free Black man—one of the very people the abolitionist movement sought to help.

Brown's men were able to capture several slave-owners but, by the end of the day, townspeople began to fight back. Early the next morning, they raised a local militia, which captured a bridge crossing the Potomac River, effectively cutting off an important escape route for Brown and his compatriots.

Although Brown and his men were able to take the Harpers Ferry armory during the morning of the 17th, the local militia soon had the facility surrounded, and the two sides traded gunfire. There were casualties on both sides.

Four Harpers Ferry citizens were killed, including the town's mayor. The militia was able to free several of Brown's captives, although men died in the fighting.

With no escape route and under heavy fire, Brown sent his son Watson out to surrender. However, the younger Brown was shot by the militia and mortally wounded.

Late that afternoon, President James Buchanan ordered a company of Marines under the command of (future Confederate General) Robert E. Lee to march into Harpers Ferry. Unable to arrange a surrender, Lee ordered the Marines to attack, taking all of the abolitionist fighters and rescuing the remaining captives.

After a 45-minute trial, Brown was found guilty of treason against the Commonwealth of Virginia and order hanged. He rode from the jail to the gallows on top of his own coffin, which was hauled in a "criminal's wagon" drawn by two white horses.

Thomas Jackson, who would later become famous as Confederate General "Stonewall" Jackson, witnessed the event. In a letter to his wife he wrote how Brown was dressed in "carpet slippers of predominating red, white socks, black pants, black frock coat, black vest & black slouch hat. Nothing around his neck beside his shirt collar."

"Brown had his arms tied behind him, & ascended the scaffold with apparent cheerfulness," Jackson continued. "After reaching the top of the platform, he shook hands with several who were standing around him. The sheriff placed the rope around his neck, then threw a white cap over his head & asked him if he wished a signal when all should be ready—to which he replied that it made no difference, provided he was not kept waiting too long."

He stood on the trap door a full 10 minutes. Finally, the order was given. The rope holding the trap door closed was sliced. "Brown fell through about 25 inches, so as to bring his knees on a level with the position occupied by his feet before the rope was cut," noted Jackson. "With the fall his arms below the elbow flew up, hands clenched, & his arms gradually fell by spasmodic motions—there was very little motion of his person for several minutes, after which the wind blew his lifeless body to & fro."

While Brown wasn't permitted to speak on the gallows, he had left a note in his cell: "I, John Brown, am now quite certain that the crimes of this guilty land will never be purged away but with blood."

They were quite prophetic words.

★

As the nation teetered on the edge, nearly torn apart by political and ideological divisions, Abraham Lincoln gave his famous "a house divided against itself cannot stand' speech.

The "house divided" line, which is drawn from the Bible, was actually part of a campaign speech he delivered at the 1858 Illinois Republican State Convention. Lincoln, then a relatively unknown politician, had just won the nomination to run for U.S. Senate against one of the most important politicians in the country, Stephen A. Douglas.

At that time, Democrats (Federalists) were the party of the slave-holding South and Republicans (anti-Federalists) were the party of the free north that opposed slavery's expansion. Yet Republicans weren't too concerned about Lincoln because they thought Senator Douglas, a Democrat, might be open to working with them against expanding slavery.

In his speech, Lincoln countered that the Dred Scott Decision the previous year had already opened the doors for slavery to be legal in the North, as well as all territories that the U.S. expanded into. If the U.S. wanted to be a free country, he argued, it had to act now before it was too late.

"A house divided against itself cannot stand. I believe this government cannot endure, permanently half slave and half free. I do not expect the Union to be dissolved—I do not expect the house to fall—but I do expect it will cease to be divided. It will become all one thing or all the other."

Fearing him too radical on slavery, the speech ended up costing Lincoln the 1858 election. Yet, he emerged from the campaign as a prominent political figure.

★

As talk of secession and war loomed large, the upcoming presidential election took center stage. The debates in Congress during this period were heated, and many members carried weapons. Southern congressmen talked openly of secession in the event of a Republican presidential victory in November.

The question of who had the power to allow or disallow slavery in the territories and the newly formed states, the federal government or the states, had been argued for decades.

The proposed admission of Missouri as a slave state in 1820, led to the Missouri Compromise. Under its terms, Maine was admitted as a free state at the same time Missouri came in as a slave state, maintaining the balance between slave and free. Additionally, Congress prohibited slavery in all western territories lying above Missouri's southern boundary.

Thomas Jefferson compared the institution of slavery to holding a "wolf by the ears, and we can neither hold him, nor safely let him go."

★

The election of 1860 was one of the most pivotal presidential elections in American history. The nation had been divided throughout most of the 1850s on questions of states' rights and slavery in the territories.

The Republican Convention was held in Chicago on May 16–18. The party, which had formed only in the 1850s, favored the abolition of slavery, but pragmatically did not call for abolition in those states that already had slavery. The divisions were apparent, as it took three ballots for Lincoln to narrowly squeeze out a victory as the party's candidate over William H. Seward, a popular former New York governor and then senator.

The Democratic Party, which had dominated politics in the 1850s, split along sectional lines, with Northern Democrats nominating Stephen A. Douglas, and adopting a platform of extending popular sovereignty to the territories.

The Southern Democrats nominated John C. Breckenridge, and their platform advocated the protection of slavery where it existed and in the territories.

Though he didn't receive a majority of the popular vote, Lincoln gained a solid majority in the Electoral College to win. Lincoln failed to receive a single electoral vote in the Deep South, where, in ten states, he was not even on the ballot.

Spurred by South Carolina, the states of the Deep South concluded that a limitation on slavery in the territories was the first step toward a total abolition of its "peculiar institution." One by one, the Southern states seceded from the Union, calling their new country the Confederate States of America and electing Jefferson Davis as its president.

Within months, John Brown's prophecy would be realized. A divided nation would be at war.

★

CHAPTER TWO
DEVIL IN A WHITE HOOD

"The limits of tyrants are prescribed by the endurance of those whom they oppress."

—FREDERICK DOUGLASS

The Civil War was the most divisive—and the deadliest—conflict on American soil.

There was nothing "civil" about it. It touched nearly every living soul in some way; it pitted families against each other; it made heroes of ordinary people and exposed the cowardice in others; it maimed and it killed without regard for race, religion or rank; it left lasting scars on a tattered nation and the South in smoldering ruins.

Over four long and grueling years the war was fought in 10,000 towns, villages, hamlets, parishes; in the dense thicket of woods, in hedge rows and open fields; house to house and barn to barn; at Bull Run (Manassas), Shiloh, Antietam, Gettysburg and Vicksburg, and places such as Peralta, Arizona, St. Albans, Vermont, Fort Ridgley, Minnesota and Santa Rosa Island, Florida.

There were small skirmishes, like at Ball's Bluff, where green Union troops of the 1st California were driven down the steep slope at the southern end of the bluff and into the river. It was like shooting fish in a barrel for the Confederates. Bodies floated downriver to Washington and even as far as Mt. Vernon in the days following the conflict.

There were large-scale battles, like Chickamauga, a Cherokee word meaning "river of death," and it was just that, where one hundred and twenty-five thousand brave soldiers met on a battlefield in mortal combat that lasted three days. When the smoke cleared, casualties were 35,000: 4,000 killed, 25,000 wounded, and 6,000 missing or captured. Gettysburg was the bloodiest battle of the war.

Union and Confederate forces totaling 160,000 collided in mortal combat at the crossroads of this tiny borough of 2,390 residents in Pennsylvania on the morning of July 1, 1863. The skies turned a glowing orangish-red as the pungent rotten-egg smell of sulfur wrought by exploding gunpower filled the air.

The battle brought unimaginable devastation to the land. Every farm, field, or garden was a graveyard. Churches, public buildings and even private homes were turned into hospitals. The two armies suffered between 46,000 and 51,000 casualties, close to one third of all troops engaged.

One war correspondent described it this way: "Every fence was knocked down, and every house or shed upon the battlefield around it had its windows shattered, its walls torn out and its roof in tatters ... The grain and grass which once grew there, was almost ground to a jelly."

The 24th Michigan regiment lost 362 out of 496 men; nearly the entire student body of Ole Miss, 135 out 139, enlisted in Company A of the 11th Mississippi were killed.

More than just numbers, these were flesh-and-blood individuals, fighting, and dying, for a cause they believed in. In letters home, the horror of battle is clear.

"Dear Wife," writes Calvin A. Haynes, a sergeant in the 125th New York Infantry. *"The 2d in the afternoon was the bloodiest part of the battle ... they opened on us ... with over a 100 cannon. We lay flat on our faces for 2 hours. The air was filled with shell bursting in every direction. The battery that lay in front of us had 55 horses and 80 men killed ... I went over the field. Such a sight I never wish to see again."*

"The stench from thousands of dead men and hundreds of horses that lay all around us is sickening," wrote Robert Cruikshank of New York State Volunteers, when describing the aftermath of the Battle of Gettysburg.

Edwin Kerrison fought at Gettysburg for the Confederate Army (Second South Carolina Infantry). He penned this letter:

"Dear Sister, on the evening of the 2nd we fought a desperate battle at Gettysburg in Pa. in which we suffered terribly being compelled to stand the fire of artillery 3 ½ hour being within the hundred & fifty yards of said battery. Our Reg. acted gloriously but has lost many a brave man ... We have only 8 or 9 men for duty in the company now ... Our Regt carried in some three hundred & odd & had 169 killed & wounded. I have not time to write particulars of the fight now as I am in haste."

★

The Civil War was fought to address two fundamental questions left unanswered by the revolution: whether the United States was to be a dissolvable confederation of sovereign states or an indivisible nation with a sovereign national government; and whether that nation, born of a declaration that all men were created with an equal right to liberty, would truly live up to those lofty principles.

The event that triggered the war came at Fort Sumter in Charleston Bay on April 12, 1861. Claiming it as their own, the Confederate army opened fire on the federal garrison and forced it to lower the American flag in surrender.

Lincoln called out the militia to suppress this "insurrection." Four more slave states seceded and joined the Confederacy. By the end of 1861 nearly a million armed men faced off against each other along a line stretching 1200 miles from Virginia to Missouri.

★

Lincoln insisted that the war was not about slavery. It was a war to preserve the Union. His words were not simply aimed at the loyal southern states. He knew most White northerners, no matter what the public rhetoric, were not willing to risk life and limb to save Blacks they didn't know.

News from Fort Sumter set off a rush by free Black men to enlist. They were turned away, however, because a Federal law dating from 1792 barred Blacks from bearing arms in the military.

As the army pushed southward, no one was prepared for the flood of slaves that would flee across Union lines. In August 1861, fugitive slaves were deemed to be "contraband of war" and declared free.

By 1862, Lincoln was considering emancipation as a necessary step toward winning the war. The South had been using slaves—men, women and children forced to build fortifications, work as blacksmiths, nurses, boatmen, and laundresses—to aid in its war effort.

The turning point for the North came when certain governments in Europe were considering recognizing the Confederacy. If Lincoln declared this a war to free the slaves, European public opinion would overwhelmingly back the Union.

Waiting for the right moment, Lincoln's chance came after the Union victory at the Battle of Antietam in September of 1862. The proclamation warned the Confederate states to surrender by January 1, 1863, or their slaves would be freed. Frederick Douglass called the act a "moral bombshell" to the Confederacy.

On New Year's Day 1863, Lincoln issued the final Emancipation Proclamation. The purpose of the Civil War had now changed. Now it was a fight to end slavery.

★

With the Emancipation Proclamation, the Union Army could officially accept Black soldiers into its ranks. All-Black units were formed.

For the most part, Black soldiers performed noncombat support functions (Black women, who could not formally join the army, nonetheless served as nurses, spies, and scouts, the most famous being Harriet Tubman). Blacks were paid as laborers rather than as soldiers—$7 per month, while White soldiers received $13 per month. Black troops strongly resisted this treatment. The 54th Massachusetts Regiment served a year without pay rather than accept the unfair wages. The War Department eventually sanctioned equal wages for Black soldiers.

It wasn't long before Black soldiers were given an opportunity to fight in the war. The Fifty-fourth Massachusetts Colored Regiment was the first authorized Black regiment. It was led by Colonel Robert Gould Shaw, a White officer born into a prominent Boston abolitionist family.

Their heroism in combat put to rest worries over the willingness of Black soldiers to fight. Soon other regiments were being formed, and in May 1863 the War Department established the Bureau of Colored Troops.

Samuel Cabble was a 21-year-old slave before he joined the 54th Massachusetts Infantry. He wrote this to his spouse:

"Dear Wife: i have enlisted in the army i am now in the state of Massachusetts but before this letter reaches you i will be in North Carlinia and though great is the present national dificulties yet i look forward to a brighter day ... great is the outpouring of the colered peopl that is now rallying with the hearts of lions against that very curse that has seperated you an me yet we shall meet again and oh what a happy time that will be when this ungodly rebellion shall be put down and the curses of our land is trampled under our feet i am a soldier now and i shall use my utmost endeavor to strike at the rebellion and the heart of this system that so long has kept us in chains . . . remain your own afectionate husband until death-Samuel Cabble."

Black soldiers served with distinction in a number of battles. In May and June 1863, Black and White Union regiments fought for the first time in major battles at Port Hudson and Milliken's Bend on the Mississippi River. Some of the White officers expressed surprise at how fiercely the Black troops fought. They didn't understand that Black soldiers were fighting for much more than restoring the Union. They were fighting to liberate their people.

A month later, Black soldiers were able to prove their fighting meddle against White soldiers, when the 54th Massachusetts Infantry led the assault on Fort Wagner, a Confederate stronghold guarding the entrance to Charleston Harbor.

Despite heavy artillery and rifle fire, the men fought heroically against Confederate defenders in brutal hand-to-hand combat. Finally driven back, the 54th suffered 40 percent casualties. Colonel Shaw was killed during the charge and was buried with his men.

Death wasn't only on the battlefield. Sickness and disease took the lives of many soldiers, both Black and White. Amos Hall was a 34-year-old Black farmer from Oxford, Ohio, who left his wife and four children to join the 54th Massachusetts. He fought in two battles before being hospitalized. The stifling heat and long marches had taken their toll on his body.

"my Deere loving and most afeconett Wife and Deer children: Good morning, I feel truly thankfull that It is threw the tender merseys of a Kind God that after A long Continuence or Dely [delay] of not writing long Before this But living in Some Hopes of Geting A ferlgh [furlough] to of [have] Gotin Home Before now, But I Hope the Presents of this letter May find you and the childrin in A Good State of Helth; But this time I am Compeld to Rite this I Know not a Plesent letter Stating that my Helth Is not At all Good, for Ever our march in florida and the Battle of olustee I Have not Bin Right Well, I Had Bin at the Hospittle At Beufort for some time from there I Came to the Regt at Morris Island Where I Got A Back Set And for the last Month or More Past I Have Suferd All But the Horid Pangs of Death, But thank the God of Heavin I feel to Be geting A Great deal Better … I Shall Rite Soon Again; I Ask youre deer Prayers; Put youre trust in god for our future Good Remember me to my deere litle ones and deere friends I Still Remain youre deer Husbent, Sargt Amos Hall"

Only a few weeks later, Amos's wife received this note:

"Mrs Hall, i sit down to pen you a few lines but it is verry painful to do it but still it is my duty to do it as a friend of your mus Most beloved Husband and as I have ben With him through all of his Sickness on Morris island Where he Was taken down and in Beaufort Where he died but i have ben sick all the time myself With the chronic diareah I have taken care of him night and day as i Would of [have] a brother … he Was buried to day the 17th i think you Can get his boddy any time you … you must Excuse my Writing as i am So Weak i cannot hardly Write my hands trembles Very bad i think of nothing more at presant … may god bless you in your trouble and afflicion From a Sincere friend of your Husband; Yours in haste, William A. Davis"

Battlefield death and sickness weren't the only enemies of Black soldiers. On April 12, 1864, an outnumbered "colored" unit of the Union Army at Fort Pillow, Tennessee surrendered. Outraged at the North's use of Black soldiers, Confederates ignored the normal rules of engagement that called for surrendering forces to be prisoners of war, instead massacring all 262 Black men, along with nearby Black civilians.

★

On March 10, 1865, Confederate soldiers in Darlington, South Carolina, arrested 17-year-old Amy Spain, the servant of a local lawyer named A.C. Spain. She was accused of "treason and conduct unbecoming a slave," because during the brief time Union troops had occupied the town, she had been a "ringleader" of the "looting," reportedly taking "linens, sheets, pillow cases, flour, sugar, lard, and some furniture" from the Spain home, where she had worked without pay and been held as property for years.

When Amy heard the sentence from her prison cell, she announced she was prepared to die. Ascending the scaffold she declared she was going to a place where she would receive a crown of glory. She was hanged under an old sycamore tree in the town square.

A month later, the war would end.

★

On April 9, 1865, General Robert E. Lee surrendered the Army of Northern Virginia at the McLean House in the village of Appomattox Court House. There were battles and clashes after this date, but for all intents and purposes the war between the States was over. The North was victorious.

Best estimates are that at least 620,000 people died (although it might have been as high as 850,000), with many more injured (there were an estimated 60,000 surgeries, three-quarters of which were amputations).

During those four years, 186,000 Black soldiers had joined the Union army (including 80 Black commissioned officers); 93,000 from the Confederate states, 40,000 from the border slave states, and 53,000 from the free states. Nearly 40,000 Black soldiers died over the course of the war, 30,000 of infection or disease.

With the war behind it, now came the long, painful process of rebuilding a united nation free of slavery.

★

Two hundred and fifty years after being snatched from their homelands, their families, their way of life, transported to an alien land, coming under conditions so appalling many would perish before reaching their destination, then enslaved like animals, dehumanized, exploited, raped, tortured and killed. Black people finally had hope that emancipation would bring true freedom and opportunity.

Forgiving in spite of all the many injustices heaped upon them, these were a people amazingly willing to live in peace with the very monsters who had done all that to them … for the promise of freedom.

As four million newly-minted Black citizens would learn, the reality was quite different. It quickly became apparent that "emancipation" did not mean "equality" for Black people. The dream turned into a nightmare of unparalleled violence and oppression.

★

On the night of April 14, 1865, only a week after the surrender at the Appomattox Court House, President Abraham Lincoln was assassinated.

That morning, well-known stage actor John Wilkes Booth, a Confederate sympathizer and White supremacist, learned the president would attend a performance of the comedy *Our American Cousin* that night at Ford's Theatre—where Booth frequently performed.

By 10:15 that evening, the comedy was well into its last act. In the Presidential Box, the president and Mary Todd Lincoln and their guests, Major Henry Rathbone and his fiancée, Clara Harris, laughed at the show along with the audience, not knowing that Booth was positioned just outside the door.

At a moment in the play Booth knew would elicit a big laugh, he burst in through the box's inner entrance, shot Lincoln in the back of the head with a .44 caliber derringer, slashed Rathbone in the shoulder with a knife, and leapt from the box to the stage below, where he exclaimed, "Sic semper tyrannis" ("Thus always to tyrants," the state motto of Virginia), then disappeared through a door at the side of the stage where a horse was being held for him. Booth would be caught and killed, and his conspirators captured and hung.

★

Andrew Johnson would become the nation's 17th president. Other than having the distinction of being born in a log cabin, he had little else in common with Lincoln. A former slaveholder from Tennessee, Johnson almost immediately issued an amnesty proclamation granting full pardons "to all white persons who have, directly or indirectly, participated in the existing rebellion."

In his first State of the Union Address, Johnson announced that he would only require the former Confederate states to accept the Thirteenth Amendment abolishing slavery in order to "resume their places in the two branches of the National Legislature" and "complete the work of restoration," and refused to require voting rights for Black people, instead leaving it to each state to decide their own electoral policies.

Taking their cue, Southern states quickly sought to re-establish enslavement by constitutional means. Johnson's action also emboldened White mobs to wage increasingly violent terror campaigns against Black people throughout the South.

★

In the immediate aftermath of the Civil War, Memphis and other large Southern cities became popular destinations for newly emancipated Blacks in search of a new life.

It wasn't long before tensions with Whites boiled over. In the late afternoon of May 1, 1866, White police officers ordered a group of Black Union soldiers in uniform who had gathered in a public park, to disperse. The soldiers refused to leave and the ensuing argument escalated into a shootout.

The violence quickly spread to other parts of the city. John C. Creighton, a city official, stirred up the White mob: "Boys, I want you to go ahead and kill every damned one of the N***** race and burn up the cradle."

For three days, enraged Whites indiscriminately beat, robbed, tortured, shot and killed 45 Black men, women, and children, injured hundreds more … and, for good measure, raped five Black women.

At least 90 Black homes were destroyed by fire, many with residents still inside, and the mobs burned down all of the city's Black churches and schools.

An editorial in *The Memphis Argus*, a White-owned newspaper, misleadingly concluded, "The whole blame of this most tragical and bloody riot lies, as usual, with the poor, ignorant, deluded blacks," then attributed the massacre to Black gun ownership.

No White people were ever held accountable for their participation in the massacres.

★

Three months later the scene would repeat itself, except this time in New Orleans at the Louisiana Constitutional Convention, which had reconvened because the Louisiana state legislature had recently passed the Black Codes and refused to extend voting rights to Black men.

A parade of 130 Black New Orleans delegates marched behind the U.S. flag toward the Mechanics Institute, where the convention was being held. A gang of

White supremacists was waiting. A shot was fired into the crowd. Fire sirens went off, signaling police—who had been sent by the mayor—to attack.

Black marchers rapidly dispersed, many seeking refuge within the Mechanics Institute. The police and a mob surrounded them and opened fire, shooting indiscriminately, then rushed the building and began to fire into the crowd of delegates, and when they ran out of ammunition and were beaten back, they regrouped, returned, and resumed firing on their mostly unarmed victims.

"For several hours, the police and mob, in mutual and bloody emulation, continued the butchery in the hall and on the street, until nearly two hundred people were killed and wounded," concluded a Congressional committee formed to investigate the massacre.

At least 200 Black Union war veterans were killed, including 40 Convention delegates. Altogether 238 people were murdered and 46 wounded. Martial law was imposed and Mayor Monroe and other city officials were forcibly removed from office for their part in the massacre—but there were no convictions.

★

While there was no justice for the victims of the riot, it galvanized national opposition to the moderate Reconstruction policies of President Andrew Johnson. Their deaths helped fuel a Northern-led Republican Party takeover of the U.S. House of Representatives and the U.S. Senate in the Congressional elections of 1866, that gave senators a super-majority, allowing them override Johnson's vetoes of radical legislation like the Civil Rights Act of 1866, the Fourteenth Amendment, and the Reconstruction Acts of 1867.

To prevent Johnson from trying to end-run them, Congress passed the Tenure of Office Act, requiring Congressional approval for any presidential removal of an executive officeholder. Johnson violated the law twice within a year. Congress proposed an impeachment resolution, which was quickly passed in the House of Representatives, as well.

Johnson's impeachment trial was characterized as "one of the last great battles against slavery"—but he was spared removal from office by one vote. He remained president for the few months remaining in the term.

★

On paper, at least, these Acts and Amendments established an equal footing for Black people. For the first time they were constitutionally protected from most forms of enslavement, recognized as United States citizens, and legally permitted to vote, to receive an education, and, in principle, to pursue the same economic opportunities Whites enjoyed.

The Black community mobilized after passage of the Reconstruction Amendments, organizing meetings, parades, and petitions calling for the implementation of their legal and political rights, including the right to vote. In 10 of the 11 former Confederate states, approximately 80 percent of eligible Black male voters were registered to vote.

During Reconstruction, an estimated 2,000 Black men served in elected office from local and state positions all the way up to Congress. Almost half of elected Black officeholders served in South Carolina and Louisiana, where Black people had the longest history of political organization. Black people also served on juries and won election to law enforcement positions like sheriff and chief of police (sometimes to fill undesirable positions or appointed as a reward for delivering Black votes).

At the same time that Blacks were participating in government in unprecedented numbers, many White elected leaders worked to undermine and substantially diminish Black political power.

In his farewell annual message to Congress, President Johnson declared that Black Americans had "less capacity for government than any other race of people," that they would "relapse into barbarism" if left to their own devices, and that giving them voting rights would result in "a tyranny such as this continent has never yet witnessed."

★

By the outbreak of the Civil War, nearly every Southern state prohibited the education of enslaved people and barred them from possessing reading material or writing instruments. Some of these laws authorized death as punishment. It was all to further the myth of racial difference rooted in the "fact" of Black inferiority and intellectual incapacity and their resulting dependence on benevolent White "masters."

Supported by the philanthropy from Northern aid societies and funding from state Reconstruction governments, Black schools quickly opened across the South. The first years after Emancipation also witnessed the creation of the nation's first Black colleges, including Howard University in Washington, D.C., and Fisk University in Tennessee.

" [A Black person] riding on a loaded wagon, or sitting on a hack waiting for a train, or by the cabin door, is often seen, book in hand, delving after the rudiments of knowledge. A group on the platform of a depot, after carefully conning an old spelling book, resolves itself into a class," noted one government official.

Black education came with a price, though. In 1870, White mobs burned "nearly every colored church and school-house" in Tuskegee, Alabama.

★

The "Redeemers" were a political movement to restore White supremacy as a foundational institution in the South. The name was a self-imposed term used by nineteenth-century southern Democrats fond of talking about "redeeming" their states from the alleged "misrule and corruption" wrought by Republican "carpet-baggers,"—viewed as Northern opportunists looking to exploit and profit from the region's misfortunes, and "scalawags,"—White Southerners who for various reasons saw more of an advantage in backing the policies of Reconstruction, and their Black allies who assumed control as Congressional Reconstruction.

The "Redeemer' movement was made up of White businessmen and wealthy planters who had enslaved Black people just a few years earlier. Immediately following the Confederate defeat, the federal government imposed restrictions that rendered these White men ineligible to vote, hold office, or otherwise exercise control over the lands and governments they had once ruled with an iron fist.

The most urgent goal was to neutralize the Black vote, which under the protection of United States troops during Reconstruction had shown astonishing power in sending Republican majorities to Southern statehouses.

"Redeemer governments," on the other hand, sharply reduced or even eliminated the programs of the state governments that benefited the poor. The public school system—that most Blacks attended—was intentionally starved for money. The care of state prisoners, people with mental illness, and the blind was also neglected; and measures to safeguard the public health were rejected.

At the same time these conservative regimes were often astonishingly corrupt, and embezzlement and defalcation on the part of public officials were even greater than during the Reconstruction years.

★

At the end of the Civil War, most Black people lived in the South, where agriculture remained the dominant industry and land ownership had long been the clearest path to economic independence and self-sufficiency.

A rumor spread throughout the South that land—over 1,000,000 acres of confiscated and abandoned farmlands—would be given to former slaves so they could own the land they had been forced to work in bondage.

"Forty acres and a mule" was, in fact, part of Special Field Orders No. 15, a post-Civil War promise proclaimed by Union General William Tecumseh Sherman to allot families, including freed people, a plot of land no larger than 40 acres (the mule was added later).

Following President Lincoln's assassination, Andrew Johnson rescinded those orders, instead returning the properties to former Confederates.

Because most formerly enslaved people lacked the cash to buy land outright, and White landowners routinely refused to provide them credit, the government's rebuff to provide targeted assistance meant that most freedmen could not build their own farms.

While some 90 percent of Black Americans resided in the South by 1870, they owned only one percent of the land.

This left Black people with few choices other than resuming toiling on plantations owned by Whites.

"There is really no difference, in my opinion whether we hold them as absolute slaves or obtain their labor by some other method," a White Alabamian remarked in 1866.

What Reconstruction ushered in, instead, then, was "sharecropping"—a new practice that soon replaced slavery as a primary source of agricultural labor and Black exploitation in the South.

Under the sharecropping system, Black laborers cleared, planted, and harvested land they did not own in exchange for a share of the crop, minus costs for food, supplies, and lodging—often in the same quarters they had inhabited while enslaved.

Even when they were paid—which didn't always happen—Black sharecroppers were almost always disadvantaged by the contracts they'd signed, many times under duress, and they were often told that their debt to the landowner was higher than their wages. This trapped many Black families in a cycle of debt for generations.

Once in debt, sharecroppers were forbidden by law to leave the landowner's property until their debt was paid, effectively putting them in a state of slavery to the landowner.

Despite these overwhelming obstacles, some Blacks did manage to acquire land and build wealth. Some—particularly those in or near larger cities—also began to open small businesses and establish themselves in various professions, such as blacksmiths, barbers, shoemakers, builders, and grocers.

In Nashville, Tennessee, in 1871, a formerly enslaved Black man named Henry Harding owned and managed one of the city's most popular hotels and built a net worth of $35,000 (over $700,000 today).

In Washington, D.C., the availability of some government jobs and establishment of Howard University created a magnet for Black intellectuals and civic leaders. Blacks who moved to the nation's capital purchased property, built successful businesses, and pursued education for themselves and their children.

★

Those were the lucky few. Many Blacks became ensnared by a new form of slavery through the criminal law—convict leasing.

As the Southern labor market faced a void left by Emancipation, Southern legislators used a loophole in the Thirteenth Amendment, which banned involuntary servitude except as punishment for crime to establish convict leasing.

After creating discriminatory "Black Codes" to criminalize newly freed Black people as vagrants and loiterers, states passed laws authorizing public officials to lease prisoners to private industries. While states profited, prisoners earned no pay and faced inhumane and hazardous working conditions. Some called it "worse than slavery."

Colonel Edmund Richardson acquired great wealth during Reconstruction, thanks to convict leasing. During the Civil War, Richardson owned five cotton plantations, but the Union naval blockade closed access to the vital New Orleans port, and he fell deep in debt. After the war, he struck a deal with Federal authorities in Mississippi (still under the rule of postwar Reconstruction), to use ex-slave prison inmates to work his farms.

When the Colonel (it was an honorary title only) died in 1886, he was the richest man in the South, and the largest cotton planter in the world, second only to the Khedive of Egypt. His estate was estimated to be worth $10 to $15 million ($260 to $400 million today).

★

If Blacks thought Washington would come to their aid, they were sorely mistaken. In fact, it made the situation worse. Congress would abandon the promise of assistance to millions of formerly enslaved Black people, and in a series of devastating decisions, the U.S. Supreme Court ceded control to the same White Southerners who used terror and violence to stop Black political participation, upheld laws and practices codifying racial hierarchy, and embraced a new constitutional order defined by "states' rights."

"A lawlessness which, in 1865 - 1868, was still spasmodic and episodic, now became organized," W.E.B. Du Bois later observed. "Using a technique of mass and midnight murder, the South began widely organized aggression upon the Negroes."

★

One of the racial boundaries protected most fiercely by White supremacists was crossing the color line on sex. For decades before Emancipation, the most fervent arguments against abolishing slavery were based on claims that freeing Black people would set off a chain of events through mixing of the races that would result in a collapse of civilization itself.

In May 1866, Tom Conyers, a Black man, was accused of offering a White girl a dime to have sex with him and repeating the proposition when she refused. As Conyers was being escorted from the courthouse to the jail in Daviess County, Kentucky, a mob including a former Confederate soldier and the girl's father seized and hanged him from a tree.

In Orange County, North Carolina in 1869, after a mixed race man named Cyrus Guy allegedly made a snide remark to a White woman, a White mob hanged him from a tree at a busy intersection and left him for days beneath a message written in blood to warn other "mullatos" to know their place. It read: "For insulting white ladies."

This argument of protecting the virtue of White women, and that interracial sex would lead to ruination, was steeped in hypocrisy (moreover, there was a strong connection between misogyny and White supremacy, where women were property, more than it being about "defense of women.").

The same communities that had lynched Black men for mere allegations of impoliteness or insults toward White women and ignored and excused White men's blatant sexual attacks against Black women and girls before Emancipation—did so afterward.

★

Across the United States, racial violence aimed at re-establishing White supremacy became widespread. In Prince Edward County, Virginia, four Black women were at home singing when a White man ordered them to stop. They refused, so he barged into the house, beat the women severely, and cut one of them with a knife. The man was fined $15.

In Georgia a White man stabbed a Black man named Andrew Price for not bringing him a cup of coffee fast enough.

Another White man shot a Black man named Hilliard Thrasher in the back for contradicting him.

A Black man named Plans Stanley was standing outside after church services in East Liberty, Texas, when a White man stabbed him, cursing, "God Damn your Black soul I will learn you to stand in the way of white ladies."

A White man in Grayson County, Texas, shot and killed a Black man named Jack Stone for failing to tip his hat.

For being rude to his White employer, Roland Carswell was beaten, attacked with a knife, and fired at with a shotgun in Dougherty County, Georgia.

Throughout the former Confederacy, White people were determined to maintain the total dominance of White supremacy and they were willing to kill to do it—believing they could act with total impunity. It's impossible to determine how many Blacks were assaulted, raped, or lynched during the Reconstruction period, but it is likely in the thousands.

In addition, the boldness and impunity with which these attacks were committed meant that many victims simply disappeared, leaving no obvious trace of their fate. The trauma of racial violence also left many Black victims and witnesses afraid to report attacks or provide testimony against White mobs and the authorities who backed them.

★

The growing wave of terror and racial violence persisted throughout Reconstruction. As White communities grew increasingly bold and confident in their ability to murder Black people without consequence, the violence expanded with the formation of organized groups like the Ku Klux Klan.

The Klan was originally a secret society—a kind of fraternal order—created in 1865 by a few ex-Confederate soldiers in Pulaski, Tennessee.

Their leadership titles were intentionally puerile: grand cyclops, grand magi, grand turk, grand scribe. Members were called Ghouls. The name Ku Klux Klan derived from the Greek word kuklos, meaning circle. Members began dressing up in sheets, apparently for publicity.

They rode around at night on horses to terrorize Blacks—reminiscent of slave patrols. The intimidating night rides were soon the centerpiece of the hooded order: bands of white-sheeted clansmen admonishing the terrified occupants to behave themselves and threatening more visits if they didn't. It didn't take long for the threats to be converted into violence against Blacks.

Before its six founders realized what had happened, the Ku Klux Klan had become something they may not have originally intended (they were willing to step outside the law, but only a little)—something deadly serious—evolving into a hooded terrorist organization that its members called "The Invisible Empire of the South," with Nathan Bedford Forrest, an ex-Confederate general, taking control as the Klan's first "Grand Wizard."

As the Klan grew, so, too, did the violence. Between 1868 and 1871, according to testimony gathered by a special investigation conducted by members of the U.S. Congress, Klansmen in just Alabama alone committed more than 100 murders and thousands of acts of violence and intimidation. These acts were not committed only by marginalized extremists. Countless White citizens participated in attacking and killing Black people.

In Warren, Kentucky, on September 5, 1868, a White mob affiliated with the Ku Klux Klan surrounded the house of William Glasgow, a Black man and former Union soldier who had pledged to vote in favor of Black rights in the upcoming election. The mob demanded that he come outside. When Glasgow refused, the mob broke into his house and killed him in front of his wife, then went to another cabin and hanged an "inoffensive negro" who had also served in the Union Army.

That fall, Prince Weaver, a prominent Black in Columbia, Florida, hosted a social gathering at his home. Five or six Klansmen fired on the group, killing 13-year-old Samson Weaver and severely wounding three others. Prince Weaver reportedly had "been warned against" holding political meetings. After learning the shots were intended for him, he fled town.

In Georgia on October 29, 1869, Klansmen attacked and brutally whipped 52-year-old Abram Colby, a formerly enslaved Black man who had been elected to Congress. Shortly before the attack, a group of Klansmen comprised of White doctors and lawyers tried to bribe him to change parties or resign from office. When he refused, the men brutally attacked him. Colby later testified before a Congressional committee.

Of the attackers, "one is a lawyer, one a doctor, and some are farmers. They had their pistols and they took me in my night-clothes and carried me from home. They hit me five thousand blows. They told me to take off my shirt. I said, 'I never do that for any man.' My drawers fell down about my feet and they took hold of them and tripped me up ... The worst thing was my mother, wife and daughter were in the room when they came. My little daughter begged them not to carry me away. They drew up a gun and actually frightened her to death. She never got over it until she died. That was the part that grieves me the most ... They broke something inside of me."

In July 1870, Klansmen killed six people, including a former missionary and then schoolteacher, William Luke. In 1869, Luke had moved to Patona, Alabama to take a job at the Talladega College, the only school for Blacks in the area. He left his wife, Fanny, and six kids behind in Grey County, saying he would send for them. He never did. Local freed Blacks identified the murderers by name during a grand jury hearing, but the all-White jury refused to indict the killers.

In Chattanooga, Tennessee, when a Black man named Andrew Flowers defeated a White candidate in the 1870 race for justice of the peace, Klansmen whipped him and told him that "they did not intend any N***** to hold office in the United States."

In 1871, 60 members of the Ku Klux Klan brutally lynched Jack Dupree, the well-respected Black president of a local political club in Monroe County, Mississippi. The mob dragged Dupree from his home. Within sight of his three young children and his wife, who had recently given birth to twins, the mob stripped him of his clothes and beat him until he was nearly dead, then slit his throat, cut out his heart and intestines, and threw his corpse into a nearby creek. His remains were never found. A witness who was forced to hold the mob's horses described the attack and recalled hearing his screams.

In York County, South Carolina, federal investigators found that nearly the entire White male population had joined the Klan.

More than 60 years later, W.E.B. Du Bois described Klan violence as "armed guerilla warfare" and estimated that, between 1866 and mid-1867, the Klan committed 197 murders and 548 aggravated assaults in North and South Carolina alone.

★

The 1868 presidential election was dominated by discussions of the Klan. Across the South, these gangs used brutal violence to intimidate Republican voters. In Arkansas, over 2,000 murders were committed in connection with the election. In Georgia, the number of threats and beatings was even higher. And in Louisiana, 1,000 Blacks were killed as the election neared. In those three states, Democrats won decisive victories at the polls.

The Klan may have been the more infamous hate group, but it wasn't the only to operate in the South.

Although Opelousas, Louisiana, in St. Landy Parish, had only 14,000 residents, an estimated 3,000 White males were members of the Seymour Knights—a branch of the White supremacist Knights of the White Camelia, which was similar to the Ku Klux Klan.

In the fall of 1868, Opelousas would be the site of one of Louisiana's deadliest Reconstruction-era massacres. Over the course of two weeks, armed White men terrorized and killed Black residents indiscriminately. An estimated 200 Blacks would die.

The brutal attacks in Opelousas terrorized Black voters into silence. One White Louisiana newspaper victoriously declared, "For the first time since the war, the negroes are polite and well disposed, and work well."

General Ulysses S. Grant won the 1868 presidential election without a single vote from St. Landry Parish.

Many Northerners, disgusted by Klan violence, lent their support to the Fifteenth Amendment, which gave the vote to Black men in every state, and the First Reconstruction Act of 1867, which placed harsher restrictions on the South and closely regulated the formation of their new governments.

In 1871, Grant signed the Ku Klux Klan Act (but not before attempting to annex Santo Domingo as a colony for freed slaves), which gave him authority to suspend the writ of habeas corpus and use federal troops to arrest and prosecute murderous Klansmen and other such organizations. Although the lynching and violence against Blacks continued, the Klan as an organization was mostly wiped out.

★

Federal efforts to address racial violence amounted to little more than establishing a committee to look into the matter. From April 1871 to February 1872, 21 Congressmen composed the imperious-sounding "Joint Select Committee to Inquire into the Condition of Affairs in the Late Insurrectionary States" and travelled throughout the South to investigate.

These proceedings yielded 13 volumes of first-hand testimony from Black and White witnesses, including state officials, former Confederate soldiers, formerly enslaved people, clergymen, teachers, and other community members.

For example, Congress heard testimony about a violent raid in Noxubee County, Mississippi. According to witnesses, a band of about 20 White men—many the county's most prominent citizens and landowners—in disguise, took over several plantations to "straighten out the N*****s."

The mob whipped 25 or 30 people in the area and shot and killed a Black man named Dick Malone who had "encouraged Black men to arm themselves and, if [the White men] came around, to give them a fight."

One of the testifying witnesses was a White man named John Taliaferro who had participated in the violence before turning informant. This raid and others, he explained, aimed to terrify Black people into fleeing the land they were renting so they'd be forced to work for the White planters.

Many Blacks who heard about the violence would leave their homes and sleep in the woods to evade roaming night raids.

Little came from the investigations. While federal officials made weak attempts to combat racial violence and Black communities tried to organize in their own defense, former Confederates worked to parlay violent terror into renewed political power.

★

Racism and violence would not be stopped by law or reason.

In August 1874, an armed mob of several hundred White men abducted 16 Black men from jail in Trenton, Tennessee, after they were accused of shooting at two White men. Six of the men were found lying along a nearby road: four were dead, their bodies "riddled with bullets," while the other two were severely wounded and later died before receiving medical attention. The other 10 Black men abducted from the jail were eventually discovered drowned at the bottom of a nearby river.

A letter published in a local newspaper from a White resident that excused the mob's murderous actions as "self-defense" and insisting that the Black men—"these incarnate devils"—had received the punishment they "richly deserve[d]." The letter declared, without evidence, that if allowed to live, the dead Black men "might [have] violate[d] the persons of a dozen ladies, burn[ed] a hundred houses and kill[ed] as many men."

When Congress passed a series of Enforcement Acts in 1870 and 1871, the broadest being the Ku Klux Klan Act of 1871, Southern White leaders used the government's own authorities against them.

They argued to the highest court in the land that the Ku Klux Klan Act was "the crowning act of centralization and consolidation" that "brushe[d] away at once and finally the all State machinery and local authority and substitute[d] in their place the Federal bayonets." In their view, federal action to punish racial violence was an unjustified intrusion on state authority, even if state governments were doing nothing to combat the racial violence themselves.

The United States Supreme Court ultimately agreed with their argument, issuing opinions that severely undermined the legal architecture of Reconstruction. While Black voters faced murder and terror, the Court was more concerned that this federal law might "fetter and degrade the State governments."

From the nation's founding to 1865, the Supreme Court had struck down just two Congressional acts as unconstitutional. Between 1865 and 1872, the Court did so 12 times.

The Court's intervention was orchestrated by John Archibald Campbell, a White lawyer and former Supreme Court Justice who had voted with the majority in the

1857 Dred Scott decision that held that Black people could not be American citizens. Campbell, himself a slaveowner, later left the bench to help lead the Confederate States of America. He bitterly opposed Reconstruction after the war's end.

When Louisiana's Reconstruction legislature implemented regulations consolidating New Orleans slaughterhouses into one location outside the city, Campbell saw an opportunity to rob the Thirteenth and Fourteenth Amendments of their purpose. He filed suit on behalf of a group of White butchers and argued that the Louisiana law forbidding slaughterhouses within city limits interfered with the butchers' livelihoods in violation of the Thirteenth Amendment's ban on slavery and the Fourteenth Amendment's "privileges and immunities clause."

By bringing cases based in facts unrelated to the Reconstruction Amendments' core purposes, Campbell hoped to use the laws as "weapons to bring about Reconstruction's ultimate demise."

The Supreme Court obliged. After consolidating Campbell's and several other cases into The Slaughterhouse Cases, the Court in 1872 held that the Fourteenth Amendment protected only the "privileges and immunities" conferred by national citizenship—a narrow category of rights mostly irrelevant to the struggles facing Southern Black people.

The majority reasoned that rights derived from a person's state citizenship were enforceable only in state courts, which were increasingly dominated by Redeemers. The Slaughterhouse Cases marked the 13th time in seven years that the Supreme Court struck down federal laws designed to protect freedmen and the decision greatly limited the Fourteenth Amendment's reach. In a dissenting opinion, Justice Stephen J. Field predicted that the amendment would be left "a vain and idle enactment."

Where Grant proved himself over and over on the battlefield, he didn't know how to contend with an enemy as stubborn as racism. As Southern racial violence became an increasingly divisive issue, a politically weakened (and often drunken) President Grant grew ever more reluctant to intervene.

Mississippi's Reconstruction Governor Adelbert Ames, a Union military veteran and a transplant from the North, requested federal troops to suppress intense White violence targeting Black communities during state elections. Grant refused and instead sent an exasperated letter encouraging Ames to broker a "peace agreement" between the state militia and the White mobs, explaining that "[t]he whole public are tired out with these annual autumnal outbreaks in the South."

Congress and President Grant also took affirmative steps to empower former members of the Confederate Army. The Amnesty Act of 1872 ended voting restrictions and office-holding disqualifications for most Confederate troops and secessionists who rebelled against the Union.

By the time of the 1872 Amnesty Act, the vast majority of White former Confederates in the South were free to own land, vote, hold office, and make laws. Only 500 Confederate leaders remained under restriction. The very same people who had so recently fought to maintain White supremacy and retain slavery were now well positioned to seize control of their state governments, create laws and policies to suppress the new civil rights of Black people, and enable continued racial terror.

★

Empowered by the Amnesty Act, Confederate veterans regained political control by espousing White supremacist rhetoric and employing terror tactics of intimidation. Confederate Colonel James Milton Smith was elected Georgia's governor in 1872 and vowed to undo the influence of post-war Reconstruction "misrule," and quickly partnered with the like-minded legislature to roll back gains that Black Georgians had accumulated under the Reconstruction administrations.

In 1874, large numbers of White supremacist candidates were elected to office in Alabama mainly due to the use of violence, threats, terror, and fraud. In Eufaula, Alabama, a branch of the paramilitary White League waged a bloody attack against Black voters to ensure White supremacist victory at the ballot box.

The Alabama election of 1874 restored former Confederate leaders to legislative and executive authority, ended Reconstruction in the state, and elected Governor George Houston. He led a political effort to reverse the aims of Reconstruction in Alabama and restore the dominance of "the great governing race—the white people of the land."

By 1875, the state legislature was controlled by White supremacists who called a Constitutional Convention to amend Alabama's "Reconstruction Constitution," ratified just seven years earlier. The 1868 Convention's 100 delegates had included 18 Black men and 79 White supporters of Reconstruction's aims.

Delegates to the 1875 Convention, by contrast, included 80 Redeemers, seven Independents, and just 12 Reconstructionists—four of whom were Black. Among other provisions, the new Constitution, ratified with more than 70 percent of the vote, mandated "[s]eparate schools ... for the children of citizens of African descent."

With many Southern governments "redeemed," White violence against Black people intensified.

On Easter Sunday in 1873, 300 White people attacked a courthouse in Colfax, Louisiana after Black protestors peacefully challenged fraudulent election results.

Even after the outnumbered Black crowd waved white flags of surrender, the assault continued and scores of unarmed Black men who sought shelter in the courthouse or attempted to flee were shot and killed.

Approximately 50 Blacks who survived the afternoon of bloodshed were taken prisoner and later executed by the White militia. As many as 150 Blacks were killed in the massacre, described as "the bloodiest single act of carnage in all of Reconstruction."

Federal prosecutors in Louisiana brought criminal charges against members of the Colfax mobs under the Enforcement Act. Despite overwhelming evidence, one defendant was acquitted and jurors failed to reach verdicts against any others. Before retrial, the defense challenged whether the federal court had jurisdiction to hear the case at all, arguing for the first time that the Enforcement Act was unconstitutional as applied to private persons who were not state actors. The court allowed the trial to proceed, but when three defendants were convicted of conspiracy, the judge ruled the Enforcement Act unconstitutional and dismissed the indictments, initiating an appeal to the Supreme Court.

In *United States v. Cruikshank*, decided on March 27, 1876, the Court upheld the lower court's dismissal and ruled that the Fourteenth Amendment protected citizens only from state action and not from violent attacks committed by private individuals.

This ruling rendered the Enforcement Act a dead letter and severely limited the Fourteenth Amendment. Blacks in the South were now at the mercy of White terrorists and had no recourse in federal courts, as long as the terrorists remained private actors.

Federal protection disappeared almost immediately after the Cruikshank decision. The Justice Department dropped 179 Enforcement Act prosecutions in Mississippi alone. Black people had few federal troops to turn to for protection, as the government had already withdrawn troops from all Southern states except Florida, Louisiana, and South Carolina. Violence grew more frequent and bolder, White mobs committed attacks on Blacks undisguised and in broad daylight.

★

In 1876, when a politically beleaguered President Grant decided not to seek a third term, Republican Rutherford B. Hayes, in a tight race that came down to the creation of a bipartisan electoral commission, just edged out a narrow victory over Democrat Samuel J. Tilden. As a concession, Hayes agreed to use his presidential authority to withdraw all remaining federal troops from the South. The "Compromise of 1877" ended Reconstruction as part of a political deal, with no inquiry into whether its goals had been accomplished.

"This is the Centennial crow that our old game rooster, who has been cooped up for twelve long years, now sings in clarion tones ... We can now shout [and] join our anthems of joy and glory with the victory of our time honored old party. Hallelujah!" the White supremacist John W. Burgess exalted. "The white men of the South need now have no further fear that the [federal powers] will ever again give themselves over to the vain imagination of the political equality of man."

The presence of federal troops in the South during the Reconstruction era acted as an impenetrable dam holding back some of the violence, political suppression, and racist rhetoric of those intent on restoring White supremacist rule. Just 12 years after Emancipation, that dam vanished.

The vast majority of Black people in America still lived in the South, where without federal protection they were at the mercy of the same White officials who had very recently waged a war to keep them in bondage. In the words of Henry Adams, a Black man living in Louisiana, "The whole South—every state in the South—had got us into the hands of the very men that held us as slaves."

On the defeat of Reconstruction, *The Nation* offered a solemn assessment: "The Negro will disappear from the field of national politics. Henceforth, the nation, as a nation, will have nothing more to do with him."

★

As a new era of White supremacy took hold in the South, accessing education became more difficult for Blacks in the face of growing hostility and dwindling resources. White employers fired Black workers for attending school and unchecked White supremacist groups like the Ku Klux Klan burned down school buildings and beat and murdered students and teachers.

In many ways, the 1881 launch of the Tuskegee Institute—originally the Tuskegee Normal School for Colored Teachers, with Booker T. Washington as its first teacher—represented a continuing Black commitment to educational achievement and the enduring commitment of White supremacists hostility toward Black education in the post-Reconstruction South.

The remarks Alabama governor and former Confederate Colonel William C. Oates gave at a Tuskegee graduation ceremony in the 1890s illustrates the point:

"I want to give you N*****s a few words of plain talk and advice," Oates began, denouncing the previous speaker. "No such address as you have just listened to is going to do you any good; it's going to spoil you. You might just as well understand that this is a white man's country as far as the South is concerned, and we are going to make you keep your place. Understand that. I have nothing more to say."

★

It was during this same period, 500 miles to the east, that Wilmington, North Carolina's largest city, develop into a bold experiment of racial solidarity in the South.

Three out of Wilmington's ten aldermen were Black, and Blacks worked as policemen, firemen, and magistrates. Wilmington even had its own Black newspaper, *The Record.*

But across the rest of state—and the South—White supremacists were working hard to reverse any advances made since the end of the war.

In 1898, just before state elections were held, Alexander Manly, the outspoken young *Record* editor, wrote that some relationships between Black men and White women were consensual. The editorial was in responded to a speech by a Georgia socialite who promoted lynching as a method "to protect woman's dearest possession from the ravening human beast."

Manly condemned lynching and pointed out the hypocrisy of describing Black men as "big burly, black brute(s)," when in reality it was White men who regularly raped Black women with impunity.

His editorial ignited White outrage across the South. There were calls to lynch him. Democrats, the party of the Confederacy, vowed to end this "Negro domination" in state legislative elections. Whites in Wilmington mobilized. They held supremacist rallies and parades and organized militias of "Red Shirts" to intimidate Blacks from voting.

Former Confederate colonel Alfred Waddell gave a speech suggesting that White citizens should "choke the Cape Fear (River) with carcasses" if necessary to keep Blacks from the polls.

On election day, the Red Shirts (a White supremacist paramilitary terrorist group) patrolled Black neighborhoods with guns. Democrats won every seat, but these were state legislative seats. Blacks still maintained power in Wilmington's city government.

Eight hundred White citizens led by Waddell met at the county courthouse and produced the "White Declaration of Independence," which stated: "We, the undersigned citizens ... do hereby declare that we will no longer be ruled, and will never again be ruled, by men of African origin."

The following day, Waddell led a mob of 2,000 armed men to the *Record* and burned the building to the ground. At the corner of Fourth and Harnett, Blacks at

Walker's Grocery Store faced off against White men at Brunje's saloon. A shot was fired. Someone yelled, "White man killed." Gunfire and violence erupted.

It quickly spread. The Wilmington Light Infantry, the White Government Union, and the Red Shirts poured into the Black neighborhoods with rifles, revolvers, and a Gatling gun.

With the battle raging, in a first-ever coup d'état on American soil, Waddell threw out the democratically-elected aldermen and installed his own. The hand-picked men, in turn, "elected" Waddell mayor.

Many Black leaders were jailed "for their own safety" and then forcibly marched to the train station under military escort and sent out of town. After the riot, thousands of Black citizens fled. In 1900, the North Carolina legislature effectively stripped Blacks of the vote through the grandfather clause and ushered in the worst of the Jim Crow laws—a collection of state and local statutes that legalized racial segregation.

★

"Chattel slavery in the United States required manufacturing a myth of racial difference to justify the brutal practice of buying and selling African men, women, and children as property," noted Jennifer Rae Taylor, a senior attorney at the Equal Justice Initiative. "The inhumanity of slavery was largely intolerable unless there was a narrative that enslaved people were not really people. The military battles and legal developments that led to the abolition of slavery did nothing to undo that project of dehumanization, and those same ideas survived to justify racial terror lynching through the criminalization of black identity."

As Reconstruction fizzled out, more and more Southern state governments quickly went to work altering their constitutions to disenfranchise Black citizens and codify racial hierarchy. From 1885 to 1908, all 11 former Confederate states rewrote their constitutions to restrict voting rights using poll taxes, literacy tests, and felon disenfranchisement.

With the last meaningful layer of federal protection removed and the Supreme Court's tolerance of extrajudicial violence, legal oppression and racial terror, lynching became defining features of Black life in America.

Moreover, local and state laws combined to trap Black people in a form of second-class citizenship by mandating segregation; outlawing interracial marriage; authorizing economic exploitation through convict leasing and mandatory labor contracts; and barring Black people from holding public office, voting in elections, or serving on juries. But perhaps the most devastating legacy of Reconstruction's failure was the deadly violence that continued to plague Black communities for decades.

The thousands of Black people killed following the war and through the remainder of the century foreshadowed the bloodshed that would persist as the ideology of White supremacy continued to strangle the hope for equality.

★

CHAPTER THREE
RAISE UP THE DEVIL

"I am only a mouthpiece through which to tell the story of lynching and I have told it so often that I know it by heart. I do not have to embellish; it makes its own way."

—IDA B. WELLS

The turn of the twentieth century was, as African-American historian Rayford Logan called it, the "nadir of American race relations,"—when racism was worse than in any other period in the nation's history. Jim Crow laws, lynching and other forms of racial violence had poisoned the society.

During Reconstruction, the presence of federal troops was able to hold back some of the violence, but with their withdrawal came a pent-up wave of unbridled lawlessness.

In 1892, a mob dragged Thomas Moss, a Black man, out of a Memphis jail in his pajamas and shot him to death over a feud that began with a game of marbles. It would have been "just another lynchin'" were it not for the fact that his godmother was Ida B. Wells, one of the nation's most influential journalists.

Small of stature—standing less than five feet tall—this former slave was a giant at battling racism using the written word. "It is with no pleasure that I have dipped my hands in the corruption here exposed," she wrote in 1892, in the introduction to her book, *Southern Horrors*. "Somebody must show that the Afro-American race is more sinned against than sinning, and it seems to have fallen upon me to do so."

Wells' personal turning point came when she bought a first-class train ticket, but was ordered by the train conductor to move to the car for Blacks. She refused on principle. She was forcibly removed from the train. Wells sued the railroad, winning a $500 settlement. This injustice led her to pick up a pen and write.

Wells saw lynching for what it was: a violent form of subjugation—"an excuse to get rid of Negroes who were acquiring wealth and property and thus keep the race terrorized and 'the N***** down,'" she wrote in a journal. "Nobody in this section of the country believes the threadbare old lie that Negro men rape white women."

It did little to stop the lynching, though. Lynching had become a tool of racial control that terrorized and targeted Blacks—it had become commonplace. It worked. It put fear into the hearts of Black people—especially to see these were often festive gatherings. Large crowds of Whites watched and participated in the Black victims' prolonged torture, mutilation, dismemberment, and burning at the stake.

When a Black man named John Hartfield was lynched in Ellisville, Mississippi, on June 26, 1919, a reported 10,000 White men, women, and children had journeyed from throughout the state to watch his gruesome murder.

Hartfield had gone to Ellisville to visit his White girlfriend, Ruth Meeks, taking a job as a hotel porter in nearby Laurel. When the relationship became known to some White men, they accused him of raping Meeks, who they claimed was 18, although she was actually in her mid-twenties. A posse of White men wounded and captured Hartfield after a ten-day manhunt.

"[Hartfield] has been taken to Ellisville and is guarded by officers in the Office of Dr. Carter in that city (his wounds were treated enough to keep him alive until his lynching)," the *Jackson Daily News* reported on June 26, 1919.

"He is wounded in the shoulder but not seriously. The officers have agreed to turn him over to the people of the city at 4 o'clock this afternoon when it is expected he will be burned."

Hartfield was hung from a tall sweet gum tree, his body then riddled with bullets, the corpse cut up for souvenirs, and what little remained was burned. Afterwards, commemorative postcards of the lynching were sent out.

Louisiana Governor Theodore Gilmore Bilbo, best known for his racist and demagogic rhetoric, declared "This is a white man's country, with a white man's civilization and any dream on the part of the Negro race to share social and political equality will be shattered in the end."

In another public spectacle, this time in Memphis, Tennessee, a mob of 25 men seized Ell Persons, a 50-year-old Black woodcutter, from a train that was transporting him to stand trial for rape and murder of a 15-year-old White girl, Antoinette

Rappel—found a half mile from Person's home. She had been decapitated with what was believed to be an axe.

The mob had announced the time and location of the lynching in advance. Many camped out overnight. By morning the roads were jammed. Some 5,000 people were in attendance. Women wore their best clothes, and parents excused their children from school.

Food and gum vendors sold their wares to the many spectators as Persons was doused with gasoline and set on fire. A 10-year-old Black child was forced to sit next to the fire and watch him die. When members of the crowd complained that Persons would die too quickly, the fire was extinguished. Two men cut off his ears for souvenirs. When he finally succumbed to the torture, his head was removed and thrown into the crowd. Attendees fought over his clothes and remnants of the rope to keep as mementos.

Edward Johnson, a Black man, was convicted of raping a White woman and sentenced to death by an all-White jury in Chattanooga, Tennessee. His attorneys appealed the case and won a rare stay of execution from the United States Supreme Court.

In response, a White mob seized Johnson from the jail—which had been conveniently vacated by the sheriff and his staff—dragged him through the streets, hung him from the second span of the Walnut Street Bridge, and shot him hundreds of times. The mob left a note pinned on the corpse that read: "To Justice Harlan. Come get your N***** now."

Through lynching, Southern White communities asserted their racial dominance over the region's political and economic resources—first achieved through slavery, would now be restored through blood and terror.

Victims were murdered for the slightest perceived offense. A Black man named General Lee was lynched by a White mob in Reevesville, Georgia, for knocking on the door of a White woman's home.

White men lynched Jeff Brown in Cedarbluff, Mississippi, for accidentally bumping into a White girl as he ran to catch a train.

In England, Arkansas, Sam Cates was lynched for the crime of "annoying white girls."

★

April 26, 1913 was Confederate Memorial Day. Most stores and businesses were closed in the South. The offices in the National Pencil Company in Atlanta, by exception, were open. Inside was superintendent Leo Frank, a young Jewish Cornell University graduate.

Thirteen-year-old Mary Phagan stopped by to collect her wages. She earned 10 cents an hour for attaching erasers to the backs of pencils.

Phagan's body was found the next day in the basement of the factory. She had a head wound and a cord was wrapped around her neck. Several strange notes were found near the body, almost incomprehensible, describing a "tall black negro." But when investigators arrived at the scene, they seized on Frank—the last man who admitted to having seen her alive.

At trial, several female workers were brought to the witness stand. They reported that Frank was sometimes known to enter the women's dressing room. Jim Conley, a Black factory sweeper who was accused of the crime in the strange notes found at the scene, was also brought in as a witness.

He, too, argued that Frank was fond of little girls, and that it was Frank who murdered Mary Phagan. He claimed to have helped carry Phagan's body to the basement. He said he had written the notes, essentially implicating himself at Frank's request.

It made no sense, but politician-turned-publisher Tom Watson had stirred up such anti-Semitism with his sensational newspaper and magazine articles, that Frank was found guilty.

The spectacle of a Jim Crow–era court relying on a Black man's testimony to convict a White man of murder was remarkable, but Frank was Jewish, so in the minds of many Southerners, he was a step lower on the evolutionary rung (it got particularly ugly when Frank's legal team, called Conley a "a plain, beastly, drunken, filthy, lying N*****" whose word should not be taken over a White man's).

The judge sentenced Franks to death by hanging. His legal team appealed and after a lengthy process it was commuted to life imprisonment. The public was outraged. A group of local men calling themselves the "Knights of Mary Phagan," abducted Frank from prison. He was summarily lynched the next morning.

Those who had succeeded in villainizing Frank at trial prospered. The chief prosecutor, Hugh Dorsey, became famous and would serve two terms as governor of Georgia; the judge, Leonard Strickland Roan, would be promoted to the Court of Appeals; and muckraking journalist Tom Watson was elected to the U.S. Senate.

It is now widely agreed that Conley committed Phagan's murder—a strange twist considering that the Klan might have liked this outcome just as well. In fact, Conley's own lawyer had insisted after the trial that he was guilty, and that Frank was innocent—a move which ended his career.

★

According to some, inspiration for awakening the Ku Klux Klan from its 40 years of dormancy, came as a result of the Leo Frank case. Frank was nothing more than a greedy, lecherous Jew preying on sweet, innocent White girls with his "Unlimited Money and Invisible Power."

It was the perfect false narrative. It also played to the ambitions of some within the organization wanting to expand from a fringe terrorist group focusing only on the "Black threat," to a robust organization hellbent on restoring the torn fabric of American life.

Most believe, however, that the revival of the KKK came about as a result of a Hollywood movie.

★

Thomas Dixon Jr. was a complicated man. He was a lawyer and legislator, as well as a celebrity preacher and writer of lurid novels that sold in the millions—which vigorously promoted ideas of White supremacy. Dixon popularized the myth of the "Black Beast" rapist and amplified stereotypes of Black men as preternaturally strong, "primitive" and inherently criminal.

His first novel, *The Leopard's Spots* (a title derived from the Biblical question: Can the Ethiopian change his skin, or the leopard his spots), tells the story of how a gang of Black Union soldiers abduct Annie Camp, daughter of a Confederate veteran, on her wedding day. The White men riding off to rescue Annie ask her father, "What shall we do, Tom? If we shoot, we may kill Annie." Tom replies, "Shoot, man! My God, shoot! There are some things *worse* than death."

Dixon followed that up three years later with *The Clansman*, which glorified the Ku Klux Klan as heroic vigilantes. The novel portrays the "ape-like" ex-slave Gus—as a "thick-lipped, flat-nosed, spindle-shanked negro, exuding his nauseating animal odour"—who rapes a 15-year-old girl.

Film director D. W. Griffith adapted *The Clansman* for the screen in "The Birth of a Nation." The three-hour silent film glorified the Ku Klux Klan as the saviors of the South from freed people, portrayed as brutish and bestial.

The Birth of a Nation was a sensation after its release in 1915. President Woodrow Wilson (a college classmate of Dixon's) praised the movie and made it the first film ever to be screened at the White House. Wilson reportedly said of the film, "It is like writing history with lightning. And my only regret is that it is all so terribly true."

Civil rights organizations, such as the recently formed NAACP, attempted to have the film banned or censored. In spite of its controversy (or maybe because of it), the film was a huge commercial success.

★

Until the movie's debut, the Ku Klux Klan was a regional organization all but obliterated due to government suppression. But The Birth of a Nation's racially-charged Jim Crow narrative—even though it greatly distorted history—coupled with America's heightened anti-immigrant climate, resonated with a wide swath of people.

William Simmons is considered to be the founder of the modern Ku Klux Klan. Simmons, a Spanish war veteran-turned-preacher-turned salesman, always dreamed of starting his own fraternal group, and in the fall of 1915 he put his plans into action.

On Thanksgiving eve, 10 days before the film was set to premiere, Simmons and a small group of his adherents climbed the massive granite dome at Stone Mountain in Georgia, set fire to a giant wooden cross, and beneath a makeshift altar glowing in the flickering flames above, laid a U.S. flag, a sword and a Holy Bible, then took an oath of allegiance to the "Invisible Empire," thus announcing the revival of the Ku Klux Klan.

"The angels that have anxiously watched the reformation from its beginnings," said Simmons, who declared himself Imperial Wizard, "must have hovered about Stone Mountain and shouted hosannas to the highest heavens."

On the movie's opening night, Simmons and fellow Klansmen, dressed in white sheets and Confederate uniforms, paraded down Peachtree Street with hooded horses, firing rifle salutes in front of the theater. Similar displays were held in other cities, including having theater ushers don white sheets.

In spite of all the hoopla, within the first couple of years, the Klan only had a few thousand members. Then Simmons met two publicists, Edward Young Clarke and Elizabeth Tyler. He gave them 80 percent of the profits from the dues of the new members.

The promoters used an aggressive new sales pitch—the Klan would be rabidly pro-American, which to them meant rabidly anti-Black, anti-Jewish, and anti-Catholic. The list of enemies would expand to include Asians, immigrants, bootleggers, dope, graft, night clubs and roadhouses, violation of the Sabbath, sex, pre- and extra-marital escapades and scandalous behavior.

With its new mission of social vigilance, the Klan soon had organizers scouring the nation, probing for the fears of the communities, then exploiting those irrational thoughts to the hilt. By the late summer of 1921, nearly 100,000 had enrolled, and at $10 a head (tax-free since the Klan was a "benevolent" society), the profits were immense.

Not stopping there, the Klan published its own national newspaper, invested in real estate, and even opened a factory to make and sell Klan robes and other products. By the 1920s the Klan had grown to somewhere between three to six million members, making it one of the largest organized domestic terror movements in U.S. history, taking political control of seven southern states.

Much of the second Klan's appeal can be credited to its militant advocacy of White supremacy, anti-Catholicism, anti-Semitism, and immigration restriction, but the organization also attracted the support of many middle-class Americans by advocating improved law enforcement, honest government, better public schools, and traditional family life. The Klan had become an accepted part of American life in the early 1920s.

As one member stated, "I never enjoyed any Lodge so much as I did the Klan. It had a principal of brotherly love for fellow members and they was a high moral tone to it."

The Klan also experienced unprecedented political gains. In 1922, Texas sent Klansman Earl Mayfield to the U.S. Senate, and Klan campaigns helped defeat two Jewish congressmen who had headed the Klan inquiry. Klan efforts were credited with helping to elect governors in 12 states in the early 1920s.

In their recruitment campaigns the Klan frequently showed "The Birth of a Nation," which not only intensified latent racism but it stirred the imagination of Klansmen longing to be equally "heroic." Sometimes that manifested itself in vigilantism, such as issuing warnings or burning crosses—an act inspired by the film, urging the offender to get out of town. "Warning parties" might beat or humiliate a victim into submission.

In Arkansas City, Kansas, Klansmen invaded "Darktown" (a term commonly used to describe the area that Black people lived in) and kidnapped a Black man who they claimed had stolen suitcases from the train station.

As the *Arkansas City Traveler* reported the next day, "To clean up this district … a group of masked men entered a negro dive and took away a negro who, it is reported, has been stealing suitcases and handbags from the Santa Fe depot and off of passenger trains. No violence took place. The men simply went in and got their man, loaded him in the rear of a Ford touring car, placed a rope about his neck, and took him on a journey to a lonely spot known as the Green lane, about three miles northeast of the city. Here they took the negro from the car and placed one end of the rope over a limb on a tree, and the noose remained about the negro's neck.

"The negro immediately dropped on his knees, pleading for mercy, and asked time to pray to his God …

after the confession, the men released the noose from his neck and told him to hit the trail. When turned loose, the negro tried to hit the trail, he tried to run and couldn't, his legs failed him for a few moments; but when he did get possession of them again, he got out of sight in a flash. It is predicted this negro will never enter Arkansas City again."

Sometimes the consequences were lethal. In 1920, Duluth, Minnesota's population was 100,000, with only 484 Blacks. Local Blacks reported that racial incidents were rare. On the afternoon of June 15, Louis Dondino drove his pickup truck back and forth along the streets of the city, shouting to onlookers to "Join the necktie party."

The night before, Irene Tusken, 19, and her boyfriend, Jimmie Sullivan, 18, both of Dondino's working class West Duluth neighborhood, attended a circus, where the couple claimed six Black circus workers robbed them at gunpoint and raped Tusken. The next morning, a physician examined the girl and determined she showed no signs of assault, yet the pair stuck to their story. Police responded by apprehending several Black roustabouts from the departing circus train, hauling six to jail.

The lack of evidence didn't deter the mob, numbering between 1,000 and 10,000 that, wielding bricks and timbers, from tearing down jail doors, yanking three of the men—Elias Clayton, Elmer Jackson and Isaac McGhie—from their cells, beating them and dragging them down the street and hanged them from a light pole, then posing for a postcard photo.

Again, no one was convicted for the murders (Louis Dondino and two other Whites were convicted for rioting only), but seven Blacks were indicted for the alleged assault. The NAACP sent attorneys to Duluth to defend them. Charges were dismissed against some, but William Miller and Max Mason were tried for the rape. Miller was acquitted, but Mason was convicted and sentenced to up to thirty years in prison (he was released after serving four years on the condition that he leave Minnesota).

★

When World War I erupted in Europe in August 1914, most Americans saw no reason for the United States to become involved. The Black press sided with France, because of its purported commitment to racial equality—chronicling the exploits of colonial African soldiers serving in the French army. Nevertheless, most Black viewed the bloodshed occurring overseas as far removed from the immediacies of their everyday lives.

The war did, however, have a significant impact on Blacks, particularly the majority who lived in the South. The war years coincided with the Great Migration, one of the largest internal movements of people in American history. Until that point, 90 percent of Blacks in America lived in the South.

Between 1914 and 1920, roughly 500,000 Black Southerners packed their bags and headed to the North—where jobs waited—fundamentally transforming the social, cultural, and political landscape of cities such as Chicago, New York, Cleveland, Pittsburgh, and Detroit.

Black Southerners faced a host of social, economic, and political challenges that prompted their migration. The majority of Black farmers, who labored as sharecroppers, lived in dire poverty. Their condition worsened in 1915 as a result of a boll weevil infestation that ruined cotton crops throughout the South.

In addition to the economic obstacles, Black people had been disenfranchised, effectively stripped of their right to vote through both legal and extralegal means, denied equal protection under the law, even forced to use separate and usually inferior facilities.

One Black Alabamian wrote in a letter to the Chicago *Defender*, "[I] am in the darkness of the south and [I] am trying my best to get out."

Wartime opportunities in the urban North gave hope and opportunity to Blacks. The American industrial economy grew significantly during World War I. Black women remained by and large confined to domestic work, while men for the first time in significant numbers made entryways into the northern manufacturing, packinghouse, and automobile industries.

"With the aid of God I am making very good [money]," wrote home one Southern Black transplant. "I don't have to work hard. Don't have to 'mister' every little white boy comes along."

Southern migrants did not always find the "promised land" they envisioned. They frequently endured residential segregation, substandard living conditions, job discrimination, and in many cases, the hostilities of White residents; but life in the North was still better for most.

"I don't care to mix with white folk. What I mean I am not crazy about being with white folks," noted one Black worker, "but if I have to pay the same fare I have learn to want to the same acomidation."

The clouds of war had reached American shores on March 1, 1917, when the Zimmermann Telegram, in which Germany encouraged Mexico to enter the war on the side of the Central Powers, became public. Wilson felt compelled to act, and on April 2, 1917, he stood before Congress and issued a declaration of war against Germany.

"The world must be made safe for democracy," he boldly stated, framing the war effort as a crusade to secure the rights of social equality and self-determination on a global scale.

Many Blacks viewed the war apathetically, but most also saw the war as an opportunity to demonstrate their patriotism and their place as equal citizens in the nation. Over one million Blacks responded to their draft calls, and roughly 370,000 Black men were inducted into the army.

Not too surprisingly, the army remained rigidly segregated and the War Department relegated the majority of Black troops to labor duties. Black soldiers served, but still had to confront systemic racial discrimination and slander from their fellow White soldiers and officers.

Racial violence quickly found its way into the war. Black soldiers were stationed and trained throughout the country, although most facilities were located in the South. They had to endure racial segregation and often received substandard clothing, shelter, and social services. In August 1917, Black soldiers of the 3rd Battalion of the 24th Infantry, stationed at Camp Logan, in Houston, Texas, had grown increasingly tired of racial discrimination and abuse from White residents, and from the police in particular.

One night the soldiers retaliated by marching on the city and killing sixteen White civilians and law enforcement personnel. Four Black soldiers died as well. The Houston rebellion shocked the nation and encouraged White southern politicians to oppose the future training of Black soldiers in the South. Three military court-martial proceedings convicted 110 soldiers. Sixty-three received life sentences and 13 received the death penalty.

The next day, the condemned soldiers (one sergeant, four corporals, and eight privates) were transferred to a barracks at Camp Travis. The condemned men were awakened at five in the morning and taken to gallows that had hastily been constructed the night before. They were hanged simultaneously at 7:17am, one minute before sunrise. The scaffolds were then quickly disassembled and hauled away. The army buried the bodies in unmarked graves.

★

The Black press and civil rights organizations like the NAACP insisted that Blacks should receive the opportunity to serve as soldiers and fight in the war. Joel Spingarn, a former chairman of the NAACP, worked to establish an officers' training camp for Black candidates. "All of you cannot be leaders," he stated, "but those of you who have the capacity for leadership must be given an opportunity to test and display it."

Howard University established the Central Committee of Negro College Men and recruited potential candidates from college campuses and Black communities throughout the country. The camp opened in June 1917, in Des Moines, Iowa, with 1,250 aspiring Black officer candidates.

The Black press vigorously debated the merits of a Jim Crow camp. W.E.B. Du Bois supported the camp as a crucible of "talented tenth" Black leadership, manhood, and patriotism.

The military created two combat divisions for Blacks. One, the 92nd Division, was composed of draftees and officers. The second, the 93rd Division, was made up of mostly National Guard units from New York, Chicago, Washington, D.C., Cleveland, and Massachusetts. The army, however, assigned the vast majority of soldiers to service units, reflecting a belief that Black men were more suited for manual labor than combat duty.

★

The war also spurred an increase in political activism amongst Black women. For the growing number of women who worked outside the home, the war created new opportunities for them to organize collectively and advocate for greater pay and equitable working conditions.

Laundresses in the South formed associations and engaged in strikes to protest unfair treatment at the hands of their White employers. In Mobile, Alabama, for example, some 250 laundry workers walked off the job (in 1917, Black laundresses made an estimated $3.00 a week, versus a national average wage of $13.00), insisting, "We are protesting against this discourteous treatment and we intend to stay out until our communications are answered and they agree to deal with our committee."

★

Over 200,000 Black soldiers crossed the Atlantic and served in France. The majority worked in service units, broadly characterized as the "Service of Supply." They dug ditches, cleaned latrines, transported supplies, cleared debris, and buried rotting corpses.

The two Black combat divisions, the 92nd and 93rd, made up of approximately 40,000 troops, did see battle. Unsure how to use Black national guardsmen, the American army "loaned" the 93rd Division to the French army. It was the only American division to serve exclusively under French command. "[The French] treated us with respect," one soldier recalled, "not like the white American soldiers." Despite having to acclimate to French methods of combat, the division's four regiments performed exceptionally well and received numerous commendations.

The 93rd Division's 369th Infantry Regiment from New York became the most famous fighting unit of Black troops. The French called them the "Men of Bronze" out of respect, and the Germans called them the "Harlem Hellfighters" out of fear.

The 369th Infantry Regiment served 191 days under enemy fire in Europe. The French government decorated the entire unit with the Croix de Guerre, its highest award for bravery, as well as 170 additional individual medals for valor, making them one of the most decorated American units of World War I.

The 92nd Division, in comparison to the 93rd, had a much more harrowing experience. Unlike the 93rd, the 92nd fought under American command. After their arrival in France, the soldiers were deployed to the front lines in August 1918.

The division saw action primarily in one of the last Allied operations of the war—the Meuse-Argonne Offensive that began in September and ended with the Armistice on November 11, 1918. Having been poorly trained and reluctantly led by White officers, the 92nd didn't fare well in combat.

Moreover, White army officials characterized Black soldiers of the division as rapists and spread vicious lies among French civilians. Black officers were particularly singled out for racist treatment because of their status. The Army later used the 92nd as justification to bar Black soldiers from future combat roles.

When the war ended on November 11, 1918, Blacks emerged from the war bloodied and scarred. What is more, Blacks fought a war within the war, as White supremacy proved to be harder to defeat than the German army.

A little over a month later, on a December morning, Charles Lewis, a returning Black soldier discharged from Camp Sherman, was headed back home. While Lewis was waiting to leave Fulton, Kentucky, the local deputy sheriff boarded his train car, looking for suspects in a robbery. He approached Lewis, demanding to inspect his baggage. The young soldier, still in uniform, declared that he had just been honorably discharged and had never committed a crime in his life. An argument broke out and Lewis was charged with assault and resisting arrest.

As news of the altercation spread, a mob of as many as 100 men gathered outside the jail. At midnight, masked men stormed the station, smashed the locks with a sledgehammer, pulled Lewis from his cell, and hung him from a nearby tree. His body, still in uniform, was left for all to see.

Days after his murder, *True Democrat*, one of Louisiana's most influential newspapers of the day, published an essay entitled, "Nip It in the Bud."

"The root of the trouble was that the negro thought that being a soldier he was not subject to civil authority," the editorial read. "The conditions of active warfare and the regulations of army life have probably given these men more exalted ideas of their station in life than really exists and having these ideas they will be guilty of many acts of self-assertion, arrogance and insolence which will not be borne with, in the South at least, and which will be followed by consequences to them, more or less painful."

As a New York newspaper wrote after the lynching, "And the point is made that every loyal American negro who has served with the colors may fairly ask: 'Is this our reward for what we have done?'"

For over two centuries, the tenuous racial status quo was based on Black people remaining subservient and "knowing their place." But now things were different. Many Blacks had labored and shed blood for democracy abroad and now expected full democracy at home. The death of Charles Lewis was the first ominous warning that not much had changed.

Racial tensions across the country would grow and translate into violence.

★

Throughout the summer of 1919, dozens of race riots erupted across the country.

The season would come to be known as the "Red Summer,"—a name coined by NAACP field secretary James Weldon Johnson, to acknowledge the blood that was shed—and would see Black populations fight back mightily against racial violence and intimidation.

Blacks were not cowed into submission, as their tormentors had hoped. Some called it the rise of the "New Negro," no longer subservient to White people. Black soldiers had returned from World War I, expecting the human rights they had fought for abroad—rights for which they were willing to die defending at home. Black veterans refused upon their return to accept injustice, inequality, and brutality by Whites.

They returned home determined to achieve a fuller participation in American society. The philosophy of the civil rights movement shifted from the "accommodationist" approach of Booker T. Washington to the militant advocacy of W.E.B. Du Bois. These forces converged to help create the "New Negro Movement" of the 1920s, which promoted a renewed sense of racial pride, cultural self-expression, economic independence, and progressive politics.

"But by the God of heaven," wrote Du Bois, who cofounded the NAACP, "we are cowards and jackasses if now that the war is over, we do not marshal every ounce of our brain and brawn to fight a sterner, longer, more unbending battle against the forces of hell in our own land. We return. We return from fighting. We return fighting."

★

The Elaine Massacre was one of the bloodiest racial conflicts of the century. It all began on September 30, 1919, at an Arkansas church in Hoop Spur, three miles north of Elaine. A group of Blacks had dared to organize a union to bring an end to the unscrupulous practices of landowners who were exploiting sharecroppers looking to collect payment for their cotton crops.

Two Black men were standing guard outside the church when three White men in a car pulled up. An argument erupted, shots were fired and W. A. Adkins, a White security officer for the Missouri-Pacific Railroad, was killed, and Charles Pratt, Phillips County's White deputy sheriff, was wounded.

Rumors of a Black uprising spread quickly. The city filled with hundreds of White men carrying guns. The local sheriff led a White posse that burned houses and schools and shot Black people at random.

H. F. Smiddy, one of the White witnesses to the massacre, swore in an eye-witness account in 1921 that "several hundred of them (Whites)… began to hunt negroes and shotting them as they came to them."

Governor Charles Brough ordered 500 Army soldiers from nearby Camp Pike—including a machine gun battalion—to march on Elaine and put down what was labeled an "insurrection" among the Black sharecroppers. Several hundred Blacks were locked up in makeshift stockades.

The White power structure in Phillips County formed a "Committee of Seven," made of influential planters, businessmen, and elected officials, to investigate the cause of the disturbances. The committee met with the governor, who accepted their authority in return for a commitment that no lynchings would take place.

The governor triumphantly returned to Little Rock the next day and told a press conference, "The situation at Elaine has been well handled and is absolutely under control. There is no danger of any lynching … The white citizens of the county deserve unstinting praise for their actions in preventing mob violence."

A grand jury in Phillips County charged 122 Black people with crimes related to the massacre. No White attackers were prosecuted, but twelve Black union members were charged with first degree murder.

"They had formaldehyde stuffed up their noses," said Krugler. "They used electrical shocks on their genitals. They were brought to court in chains and not allowed to see an attorney. They were quickly convicted and sentenced to death [in the electric chair] within [six] minutes." As a result, sixty-five other Blacks charged with lesser crimes quickly entered plea-bargains and accepted sentences of up to twenty-one years.

RAISE UP THE DEVIL

★

The account that best captured the Elaine Massacre came from Ida B. Wells. She dressed up as a sharecropper and went to Arkansas where she interviewed the prisoners and many others, publishing her findings in a 1920 pamphlet.

One union member, Ed Ware, told of how White men had fired into the Hoop Spur church, killing several people, then burned it down the next day with bodies inside. When he returned home, 150 men came to ransack his house, seizing his union meeting minutes and his Masonic lodge books. As they surrounded his house, another man inside, Charlie Robinson, tried to run away. He was elderly and handicapped, and ran too slowly. They shot him and left him to die. They stole Ware's cow, two mules, one horse, a farm wagon, his Ford car and various household goods. He lost 121 acres of cotton and corn.

Many families described how they had run into the woods for safety from bloodthirsty mobs, hoping to surrender themselves to the federal troops for safety. Instead, the troops either shot or arrested them.

Vigilantes from Mississippi seized another union member, Lula Black, and her four children from her house, knocked her down, pistol whipped and kicked her, then took her to jail.

The mob then moved to another home, where they murdered Frances Hall. In a final act of disrespect, they tied her dress over her head and left her body on the side of the road for several days.

When the wife of Frank Moore, who had hidden for four weeks, returned home, a plantation manager-neighbor, Billy Archdale, told her "if she did not leave, he would kill her, burn her up, and no one would know where she was." Most of those who survived found their homes emptied of possessions that appeared in White peoples' houses.

In *Moore v. Dempsey*, the high court in 1923 overturned the convictions of six of the Elaine 12 in a 6-2 ruling, arguing that the confessions had been secured through torture. The trial had occurred in a setting dominated by a mob spirit, violating the prisoners' right to due process.

The decision by the justices was aided by two White men involved in the massacre who reversed their previous testimonies, acknowledging that the planters had gone to the Hoop Spur church to destroy the union and that the posse had killed their own men, instead of the Black people who had been accused. They went on to describe the wholesale massacre of hundreds of unarmed and defenseless Black people, and the torture used to secure confessions.

Two years later, the other six on death row and those in prison on lesser charges all had their sentences commuted.

It is impossible to establish an accurate death toll from the massacre. Military reports were intentionally vague. Local authorities blocked press coverage. Estimates have ranged from 25 to over 800.

★

A four-day riot in Washington, D.C. began on July 19, 1919, when a rumor that Black men had assaulted a White woman incited mobs to attack local Black neighborhoods. As the *Washington Post* reported, 19-year-old Elsie Stephnick was walking home from her job at the Bureau of Engraving when two Black men allegedly collided with her and tried to steal her umbrella.

The police arrested Charles Ralls, a Black man, for the alleged attack, but he was quickly released. By then, however, the tale quickly grew taller with each telling, and before long, four daily newspapers, in a heated war for readers, fueled the fire with headlines like the *Washington Post's* "Negroes Attack Girl. White Men Vainly Pursue" and the *Washington Times'* "Negro Thugs."

Stephnick's husband, a Naval Aviation Corps employee, became convinced Ralls was one of the men responsible for attacking his wife and before long had gathered more than 100 servicemen who, after hours of heavy drinking, "brandishing pipes, clubs, sticks, and pistols," marched south across the Mall to a poor, black neighborhood then known as Bloodfield.

"A mob of sailors and soldiers jumped on the [street]car and pulled me off, beating me unmercifully from head to foot, leaving me in such a condition that I could hardly crawl back home," said Francis Thomas, a Black 17-year-old. Thomas said he saw three other Blacks being beaten, including two women. "Before I became unconscious, I could hear them pleading with the Lord to keep them from being killed."

Newspapers continued to stoke the flames of hatred—with alleged sex crimes by a "negro fiend"—and falsely reporting that 500 revolvers had been sold at pawn shops.

When the Metropolitan Police Department finally arrived in force, its White officers arrested more Blacks than Whites, sending a clear signal about their sympathies.

Over four days, Washington, D.C. became a battlefield. "Race war galloped wildly through the streets of Washington last night, reaping a death toll of four and a list of wounded running into the hundreds," the *Washington Times* reported. "Bands of whites and blacks hunted each other like clansmen throughout the night, the blood-feud growing steadily. From nightfall to nearly dawn ambulances bore their steady stream of dead and wounded to hospitals."

President Woodrow Wilson ordered 1,000 federal troops into the city to quell the violence. Nine people were killed in brutal street fighting, and an estimated 30 more would die eventually from their wounds. More than 150 men, women and children were clubbed, beaten and shot by mobs of both races. Several Marine guards and six D.C. policemen were shot, two fatally.

★

Events in Washington were closely followed by a massive race riot in Chicago.

Like a number of big Northern cities, Chicago was experiencing the first of several waves of migration—its Black population doubled between 1915 and 1920. White discharged military personnel returned home to find themselves in competition with Blacks for industrial jobs in the South Side's steel mills and stockyards.

Black laborers already suffered from the stereotype of low wage-earning strikebreakers, or "scabs," who would keep factories in operation while employees went on strike. Whites also worried about the Black voters aligning with Republicans to swing votes in their favor.

White newspapers resorted to dialect and minstrel-like scenarios to demean Blacks and discredit their claim to housing and job opportunities. Black papers stressed a worsening climate of racial violence locally and nationally, often to sensationalized extremes, and denounced the unwillingness on the part of city authorities, especially the police, to protect Blacks' rights.

By 1919, Black homeowners and renters were concentrated in a narrow band of the South Side of Chicago that came to be known as the "Black Belt." Hyde Park, which was just south of the Black Belt, was one of the most intolerant neighborhoods. Property owned by a wealthy Black businessman named Jesse Binga was bombed six times.

Mary Bryon Clarke, another Black homeowner, had her properties targeted by bombs three times, even though the previous White owners of two of her buildings had run them as brothels.

In the summer of 1919, Chicago was in the throes of a brutal heatwave. Thousands flocked to the beaches lining Lake Michigan for some relief. Among them was a group of Black boys that included 17-year-old Eugene Williams. Williams, who was on a raft, inadvertently drifted over the invisible line into a "Whites only" area. One White beachgoer, insulted, began throwing rocks at the Black kids. Williams slipped off his raft and drowned.

Anger escalated when it became apparent that no arrest would be made. More police arrived. One especially distraught Black beachgoer pulled out a gun and fired into a knot of police. He was shot dead immediately.

Several groups of young White men climbed into cars and began racing through streets in the city's Black neighborhoods, randomly firing at homes and businesses. Others armed themselves with guns, sticks, and rocks and began marching up 35th Street, assaulting any Black person unfortunate enough to cross their path.

When the smoke cleared and the ashes cooled, 38 people—23 Black, 15 White— were dead. More than 350 people reported injuries. In Chicago, some 1,000 Black homes had been burned down. None of the White participants in the riot ever faced consequences for their involvement.

As bad as the killing was, it was only a manifestation of much deeper and darker factors at work prodding the city and a nation toward violence.

★

By the early part of the twentieth-century lynching had become so commonplace in America that, in 1918, Representative L. C. Dyer of Missouri introduced a bill in the House of Representatives to make lynching a federal crime.

The bill went nowhere, so it was reintroduced in 1921. The legislation became one of the NAACP's central goals. It a NAACP report, *Thirty Years of Lynching in The United States: 1889-1918,* noted, "The United States has for long been the only advanced nation whose government has tolerated lynching."

Sixty-two pages of the 113-page report is a single-spaced list of the 3,224 confirmed lynchings during that period, some 80 percent of which were of Blacks. The report also highlights 100 of the lynchings, among them:

"Bailie Crutchfield, a colored woman, was lynched by a mob at Rome, Tennessee because her brother stole a purse."

"Sam Hose, a Negro farm laborer, was accused of murdering his employer in a quarrel over wages. He was burned at the stake … Before the torch was applied to the pyre, the Negro was deprived of his ears, fingers and other portions of his body with surprising fortitude. Small pieces of bone went for 25 cents and a bit of the liver, crisply cooked, for 10 cents."

A mob, formed near Liberty County, pursued through seven counties a Negro supposed to be Ed Claus, who had assaulted Susie Johnson, a young White woman, and lynched him, hanging him and shooting him full of holes. After he was lynched it was found he was not Claus."

"Just at sunrise this morning two local Negroes took the hemp cure for propensity to insult white women."

As if turning a blind eye to lynching wasn't bad enough, most of the time the press blamed the victim. In 1921, *The Ocala Evening Star* defended lynching by claiming that a mob victim, Elijah Jones, was a "bad N*****" and a "degenerate young devil." The paper went on to argue that the lynch mob was made up of "representative citizens, and they consider it their duty to rid their country of rapists and rattlesnakes as soon as possible."

An article in the *Gainesville Daily Sun* blamed the events in Rosewood on a "brutish negro" who "made a criminal assault on an unprotected white girl."

★

The Dyer Anti-Lynching Bill passed the U.S. House of Representatives on January 26, 1922, but its approval was halted in the Senate by a filibuster by Southern Democrats, who formed a powerful block. They argued that lynchings were a response to rapes and therefore should be left for states to deal with.

The election of Franklin D. Roosevelt in 1932 was expected bring an end to lynching. That same year, Democratic Senators Robert F. Wagner and Edward Costigan agreed to draft an anti-lynching bill. The legislation proposed federal trials for any law enforcement officers who failed to exercise their responsibilities during a lynching incident. Roosevelt refused to speak in favor of the bill. He argued that the White voters in the South would never forgive him.

Even the appearance in the newspapers of the lynching of Rubin Stacy failed to change Roosevelt's mind on the subject. Stacy was being escorted by six deputies to Dade County jail in Miami on July 19, 1935, when he was taken by a White mob and hanged by the side of the home of Marion Jones, the woman who had made the original complaint against him.

The *New York Times* later reported that "subsequent investigation revealed Stacy, a homeless tenant farmer, had gone to the house to ask for food; the woman became frightened and screamed when she saw Stacy's face."

In 2018 the Senate passed the anti-lynching legislation Justice for Victims of Lynching Act, on which the House of Representatives took no action. On February 26, 2020, just over 100 years after the original bill was introduced, the House passed a revised version, the Emmett Till Anti-lynching Act, by a vote of 410–4 (the four dissenting votes coming from three Republicans and a Libertarian).

As of the writing of this book, the bill is still being considered by the Senate, with Kentucky Republican Senator Rand Paul opposing the bill's language for being "overly broad,"—meaning there is currently no federal law on the books in America specifically outlawing lynching.

In the words of historian Robert Zangrando, anti-lynching legislation was "displaced by the indifference of its friends and the strategy of its enemies."

★

On May 30, 1921, a young Black teenager named Dick Rowland entered an elevator at the Drexel Building, an office building on South Main Street in Tulsa, Oklahoma. The doors closed, the young White elevator operator, Sarah Page, screamed, Rowland fled.

The police were called, Rowland was arrested. By the time it hit the afternoon newspapers, a front-page story claimed that Rowland had sexually assaulted Page. As evening fell, an angry White mob gathered outside the courthouse. They demanded Sheriff Willard McCullough hand over Rowland. He refused, and had his men barricade the top floor to protect the Black teenager.

When rumors started flying of a possible lynching, a group of around 75 armed Black men came to the courthouse shortly after 10:00pm, where they were met by some 1,500 White men, some of whom also carried weapons. A struggle ensued and a White man was shot, sparking the murderous rage that would follow.

Over the next several hours, groups of White Tulsans—some of whom were deputized and given weapons by city officials—committed numerous acts of violence against Black people, including shooting an unarmed man in a movie theater.

Walter White, who later became executive secretary of the NAACP, said, "One story was told to me by an eyewitness of five colored men trapped in a burning house. Four were burned to death. A fifth attempted to flee, was shot to death as he emerged from the burning structure, and his body was thrown back into the flames."

There were reports that White men flew airplanes above Greenwood (a section of the city made up primarily of middle-class Black families), dropping kerosene bombs. "Tulsa was likely the first city" in the U.S. "to be bombed from the air," according to a report by the Oklahoma Commission to Study the Tulsa Race Riot of 1921.

"The sidewalk was literally covered with burning turpentine balls," B.C. Franklin, a lawyer in Greenwood wrote. "For fully forty-eight hours, the fires raged and burned everything in its path and it left nothing but ashes and burned safes and trunks and the like that were stored in beautiful houses and businesses."

Whites killed more than 300 Black people—dumping their bodies into the Arkansas River or burying them in mass graves. More than 1,200 Black-owned houses burned. Two newspapers, a school, a library, a hospital, churches, hotels, stores, and many other Black-owned businesses were among the buildings destroyed or damaged by fire.

By the time the National Guard arrived and Governor J. B. A. Robertson declared martial law shortly before noon, the riot had effectively ended. Though guardsmen helped put out fires, they also imprisoned many Black Tulsans, and by June 2, some 6,000 people were under armed guard at the local fairgrounds.

In the hours after the Tulsa Race Massacre, all charges against Dick Rowland were dropped. The police concluded that Rowland had most likely stumbled into Page, or stepped on her foot. Kept safely under guard in the jail during the riot, he left Tulsa the next morning and reportedly never returned.

Two weeks after the massacre, the Tulsa City Commission issued a report blaming the destruction on the Black people who lived there, not the White mob that pillaged, plundered, and destroyed Greenwood.

"Let the blame for this Negro uprising lie right where it belongs—on those armed Negroes and their followers who started this trouble and who instigated it and any persons who seek to put half the blame on the white people are wrong," according to the commission.

The *Tulsa Tribune's* editor, Richard Lloyd, was more direct: "But there is a bad black man who is a beast … He drinks the cheapest and the vilest whiskey. He breaks every law to get it. He is a dope fiend. He holds life lightly. He is a bully and a brute."

Tulsa's White churches echoed similar sentiments. "The fair name of the city of Tulsa has been tarnished and blackened by a crime that ranks with the dastardly deeds of the Germans during the Great War, provoked by the bad element of the negroes, arming themselves and marching through the streets of the city. Block after block of our city has been swept by fire, applied by the frenzied hand of the mob, many of our people are dead, while thousands of innocent, peaceable, and law-abiding citizens have not only been rendered homeless, but they have been robbed and despoiled of all their earthly possessions. The pastors of Tulsa blush for shame at the outrage which renders our city odious and condemned before the world."

The Red Cross, which was called in to help, wrote a report detailing its findings. "[Some have] referred to the affair as a 'race riot,' others with deeper feeling refer to it as a 'massacre,' while many who would saddle the blame upon the negro, have used the designation, artfully coined, 'Negro-up-rising.' Whatever people choose to call it the word or phrase has not yet been coined which can adequately describe the events of June 1st.

"The elements of 'race rioting" were present, from all evidence, on the night of May 31st, but the wholesale destruction of property—life and limb—in that section of the city occupied by negroes in June 1st between the hours of daylight and noon testifies to the one-sided battle … All that fire, rifles, revolvers, shot guns, machine guns and organized inhuman passion could do with thirty-five city blocks with its twelve thousand negro population, was done … A heavy pall of smoke kindly mantled the ruins for the first twenty-four hours, during which time Tulsa had rubbed her eyes and prepared to face a condemning world."

★

The riots in Washington, D.C., Chicago and Tulsa, were tragic, but those cities would rebuild and find a way to move on, especially the Black citizens.

For instance, in a Red Cross Relief Board report on the Tulsa Riots, the committee noted, "The courage with which Tulsa Negroes withstood repeated attempts of the city administration to deliver the "burned area" over to certain land grafters is the subject of most favorable comment all over the country. The rapidity with which business buildings and residences are being rebuilt, in most instances, better than before is proof in wood and brick and stone, of the black man's ability to make progress against the most cunningly planned and powerful organized opposition."

★

The atrocity that happened just over a year later in Rosewood, Florida would not end with any hoped-for better future.

Instead, it would become an unseen reminder of America's shameful past, one that whose flames would burn brightly well after the fires of Rosewood were extinguished.

★

CHAPTER FOUR
ROSEWOOD MASSACRE

"Let it be understood now and forever that he, whether white or black, who brutally assaults an innocent and helpless [White] woman, shall die the death of a dog."

—THE GAINESVILLE DAILY SUN, 1923

In 1513, while in search of the fabled fountain of youth, Spanish explorer Ponce de León landed on the American peninsula, near present-day St. Augustine, and claimed it for his Queen. It was during the Easter season, so he called the land Pascua Florida (Festival of Flowers).

The first Blacks to touch Florida's shores were likely part of his crew, which included several free Blacks. One of them, Juan Garrido, a native of West Africa, later participated in Hernando Cortés's 1519 defeat of the Aztecs and conquest of Mexico, and was the first person to grow wheat in the Americas.

The first recorded Black slaves to reach "La Florida" arrived in late September 1526, as part of the Lucas Vázquez de Ayllón expedition. As many as 100 slaves helped to establish a new Spanish settlement, which he named San Miguel de Gualdape (near present-day Sapelo Island, Georgia). The short-lived colony endured for less than two months, before many of the slaves rebelled and the settlement was abandoned.

Less than two years later, in 1528, conquistador Pánfilo de Narváez mounted an expedition into La Florida. Word of the riches earned by Cortés made finding volunteers easy. Onboard one of five ships manned by some 600 Spanish soldiers and adventurers, was Esteban de Dorantes, a Moorish slave and highly-regarded scout, who took part in an extraordinary eight-year odyssey across the North American continent in search of the "Seven Cities of Gold." He would be the first enslaved non-native man to visit the vast southern reaches of the Colorado Plateau in today's Arizona and New Mexico.

★

In 1565, Spanish explorer Pedro Menéndez de Avilés established the first permanent European settlement in Florida, at what today is known as St. Augustine. They would find an almost unbroken forest.

Swiss-born Francis Philip Fatioorn had been a soldier for France, a viscount in Sardinia and a merchant in London, before chartering a vessel in 1771 to sail with his family to St. Augustine, where he started plantations to cultivate indigo, extract turpentine, plant orange groves, and raise sheep. He was one of the first to recognize the value of Florida's forests. He wrote back home to tell of the wonders of the land.

"The yellow pine of East Florida is remarkably large, straight and of fine grain—rather heavy for single stick or large mast. For made masts, I humbly apprehend, it would be very proper as it is easy to find large trees free of all kinds of knots—from 40 to 50 feet in length—for deck planks no wood is equal to it. I had some sawed above 40 feet, free of knots and clear of heart shake (cracks in the wood)."

★

Levy County, Florida was formed in 1845, following the Seminole Wars—when most Native Americans were either killed off or forcefully driven out of the state. The county was named for David Levy Yulee, a Sephardic Jew who ran a 5,000-acre sugar cane plantation using Black slave labor—before it was destroyed in the Civil War. When Florida was admitted into the Union in 1845, Yulee became the first Jew in the United States to win a seat in the Senate.

1845 also saw the establishment of Rosewood—by a handful of White settlers who homesteaded large tracts of land in the swampy wilderness. Located in western Levy County, nine miles from the Gulf of Mexico. Rosewood took its name from the over 10,000 acres of abundant red cedar that grew in the area. By 1855, seven homesteads were strung out along a dirt trail leading to Cedar Key.

By 1870, the market value of cedar and the commercial production of oranges, as well as vegetable farming and limited cotton cultivation, justified a railroad station and small depot at Rosewood.

The cedar was cut and then shipped by rail to Cedar Key on the Seaboard Airline Railway and processed there at two large international pencil mills—J. Eberhard Faber and the Eagle Pencil Company. The finished timber was then sent by boat to New York factories and fashioned into lead pencils.

Rosewood had about a dozen two-story wooden plank homes, other small two-room houses, and several small unoccupied plank farm and storage structures. Some families owned pianos, organs, and other symbols of middle-class prosperity.

Years later, a former-Rosewood resident remembered it as a happy place. "Everyone's house was painted. There were roses everywhere you walked. Lovely."

The county opened a school for Whites, and soon there was a privately owned hotel and post office. Whites established a Methodist church in 1878, and Blacks followed in 1883, with their own African Methodist Episcopal church. Pleasant Hill, a second AME church, was founded in 1886.

Although the hamlet became a small village, Rosewood was never incorporated.

By 1890, due to overharvesting of the timber, most of the red cedar had been cut out. The final blow was the hurricane of 1896. The eye of the powerful and destructive cyclone pushed directly into the Cedar Key—intense 125 mile an hour winds traveling 35 miles an hour—sent a ten-foot wall of water rushing over the banks, invading every building in town, leaving large sinkholes when it receded.

Sidewalks along streets were washed out, the surge of water undermined the foundations of stone buildings, weakening many of them to the point of collapse, while sweeping away weaker structures. Inside buildings left intact, mud was found several feet deep. A fire broke out during the storm and reduced two large Cedar Key hotels to mounds of coquina.

The devastating forces continued inland over the Suwannee River valley, causing widespread destruction in dozens of communities across interior northern Florida. It razed 5,000 square miles of dense pine forests, transforming the landscape, giving it a "prairie-like appearance, "crippling the turpentine industry" (at the time, the second leading industry in Florida) and enfeebling the pencil industry, leaving its future in doubt.

Working its way northward, through Georgia, the Carolinas, Virginia, West Virginia, Washington, D.C., Maryland, Pennsylvania, New Jersey, and New York, before turning westward, Hurricane Number 4 (this was well before the National Hurricane Center started officially naming hurricanes in 1950) cut a path through the Great Lakes, reaching as far as the Lake Michigan shores, where eight days later, it was still powerful enough to tear a schooner from its moorings at Chicago and toss it into nearly a dozen smaller vessels, while a barge broke up and capsized near Milwaukee, taking the lives of four crew members. By the time it was over, the death toll climbed to over 200.

★

By 1900, Rosewood had seen the White families move out, leasing or selling their land to Blacks. The post office and school closed, relocating to the site of a new cypress mill that opened in Sumner, a village three miles west of Rosewood.

Some Blacks were able to find employment there, but many worked for the Black-owned M. Goins & Brothers' Naval stores company in Rosewood. The company was owned by three brothers—Edmund, Lucian and Matine—sons of Lucy Goins, from Moore County, North Carolina. The company prospered by distilling turpentine and rosin obtained from the large tracts of pine trees growing nearby. At its peak the Goins brothers' operation owned or leased several thousand acres of land.

Facing a number of lawsuits from competing White firms that owned their own small lumber and turpentine operations—harassing the company and the workers, filing complaints for everything from trespassing to damaging timber—the Goins family terminated their operations, and by 1916 had moved to Gainesville in adjoining Alachua County, taking the jobs with them.

But Rosewood survived. A few Black-owned businesses continued to operate. Some in town made their living by small scale farming and by trapping in the vast Gulf Hammock that surrounded the area. A number of Rosewood's Black women worked in Sumner as part-time domestics for White families.

By 1920, Rosewood had three churches, a train station, a large Black Masonic hall, where the second floor served as a school for the Black children, with Mrs. Mahulda Brown-Carrier as the teacher (provided they had the 15 cents a week tuition). It even had its own baseball team, the Rosewood Stars.

There had never been much trouble to speak of between the people of Rosewood and Sumner. Black and White children from both towns would often play in the woods together, chasing rabbits, stalking snakes, and picking wildflowers.

★

In 1922, In addition to their operation in Sumner, Cummer Sons Cypress Co. built a modern, fully electric cypress sawmill and box factory in nearby Lacoochee. The mill was used to cut the company's cypress, pine, and hardwood timber holdings in central Florida.

Jacob Cummer, founder of the lumber empire, had worked in his father's mill in Canada and eventually formed his own company, purchasing tracts of timber in Michigan. In the 1880s, the lumber industry prospered there, but by 1893, the supply of timber was depleted, and Cummer sought other properties.

Under grandsons Arthur and Waldo and their brother-in-law, J.L. Roe, the Florida operation was booming, cutting 60,000 board-feet of lumber a day.

Arnett Goins, whose father was a stacker up at the Sumner mill, remembers, "The Cummers lived in a mansion up at the other end of town, across the tracks, a huge three-story home like something out of the movies, set back behind the moss-hung oaks, surrounded by hundreds of acres of private woods loaded with fish and game, patrolled by armed guards who arrested anyone caught trespassing. Before they took you to jail, they would give you a good beating just to make sure this wouldn't happen again."

★

Thirty-year-old Henry James Taylor—he went by James—a skilled millwright, worked at Cummers (as the locals called it) in Sumner.

Cummers wasn't the only employer in the area. Some men worked in the remaining turpentine camps, stoking the fires. Back then, turpentine's primary products were tar and pitch—both needed to seal ships (to preserve ropes and rigging on sailing ships and to caulk the seams between timbers in the ships' hulls), but turpentine was used in numerous products as well, from lamp "oil," soap, lubricants to medicines. Vicks VapoRub originally contained turpentine.

Some went deep into the woods, loggers felling the trees that would feed the mills. It was tough work, and it was dangerous: twelve hours a day, standing in waist-high swamp water, working with mighty seven-foot cross saws—making as much noise as possible to keep the alligators away and hoping the water moccasins would seek out other prey—searching out trees thousands of years old, some six feet or more wide at the trunk (some ran 90 feet in height before you even got to the first limb), then once conquering these beasts, having to snake the timber back through the dense forest to the waiting trains that would haul them to the mill.

Then there were the fur trappers, running their lines for mink, otter and coon. French explorer Jacques Cartier in his three voyages into the Gulf of St. Lawrence in the 1530s and 1540s conducted some of the earliest fur trading between European and First Nations peoples. John Jacob Astor, the first millionaire in the United States, made his initial fortune in the fur trade, but by the turn of the twentieth century, as demand fell and many species were nearly eradicated, it was a way to eke out a living and put food on the table.

Working at Cummers was certainly a plum job and James Taylor was considered a valued employee.

As was his custom, he left the house in darkness for the lonely walk to the mill. His wife Fannie and their two children still asleep in their beds. His job was to coax the stiff saw blades back to life each morning, loosening the giant wheels of notch-toothed steel with squirts of oil.

By 7:00am, many of the mill's White employees trudged off for that Monday morning shift, signaled by the roaring whistle off in the distance. It didn't matter that it was New Year's Day. Stacks of cedar and cypress waited to be cut down to size.

Others took the log train several miles out into the Suwannee swamps, where they would camp in the wet, bug-infested woods for the week (sleeping in special-ly-constructed boxcars), harvesting trees, before returning Saturday night. Some trudged to the nearby railroad whistle stop called Wylly, to stoke the turpentine stills and wheedle the conifers into giving up their sticky amber resin.

The pine groves muzzled most of the noise of the mills, except for that occa-sional stubborn log that when it hit the big saw put out a yelp, like the faint, raspy sound of a mockingbird. Before long, it was silent again, except for the sporadic dog barking.

★

Within a few hours, Sumner was coming alive. The daybreak sun was peeking through the treetops. You could smell biscuits baking—likely at Mrs. Cannon's house. Nothing tasted better, especially with a spoonful of home-cooked cane syr-up on top. Virginia Hudson's milk cow was mooing, as usual. Grace Pillsbury was doing what she did every morning, after her devotional reading from the Good Book, she was sweeping the dirt from her back porch, lost in thought, when, out of nowhere, came that frightening scream.

Who could forget that sound? It was a jagged shriek that penetrated the morn-ing calm. Then another, followed by incessant heaving sobs that seemed to cry out in pain.

There was Fannie standing in her front yard, awkwardly lost, like a child waking up from a nightmare, trembling whimpers escaping her lips only interrupted by the need to draw breath, when several neighbors rushed over.

Francis Smith reached out to comfort her. Fannie reflexively jerked back. "Some-one needs to grab up my babies!" Fannie hollered. "That N*****'s still here!"

She then fainted.

★

In Fannie Taylor's version of the events, a Black man knocked at the door, and when she opened it, he burst in, pushed her, knocked her to the floor, and then proceeded to "assault" her.

"She opened the door, and, well he done knocked her down and she was raped," said then 16-year-old Edith Foster.

According to two eyewitnesses, though, that's not what happened. Fannie, they say, had a lover, a White man. He was the one who assaulted her.

"We was workin' for Miss Fannie. I works for a bunch of them white women in town," said Sarah Carrier, a Black woman from nearby Rosewood who walked the three miles each Monday to do laundry for some of the White women in Sumner.

Sarah's husband, Haywood, had suffered two strokes. Incapacitated for mill work, he earned his living trapping and selling hides. To supplement their meager income, Sarah did chores and occasionally sold eggs and vegetables at the Rosewood railroad station.

"I do washin' and ironin'. I had Philomena (her granddaughter) wit me that day to help with stackin' the wood.

"We was makin' a fire for the boilin' pot when we hear the train come down the track. We knew from before that Miss Fannie was goin' have her a visitor. Her husband, he worked at the sawmill. He was workin'.

"This gentleman walks up from the woods, opens the gate, right by where we is and walks into that house. He was white. We see'd him before.

"After a while they got to arguin'. I don't know what they was arguin' about, but it got loud. I walked over to where I could see in the window. She done slapped his face. Just like that. Slap him hard. They stopped arguing. I went back to the boilin' pot.

"A few minutes later the man comes out the house. He was holdin' his face as he walked on past. Real matter factly, wasn't in no hurry, then he took to running toward the tracks.

"Miss Fannie she come out the house a little while later. Maybe thirty minutes later. About that or a little more. She come out and was screamin'.

She must have noticed the condition she was in because she was talkin' 'bout how she'd been attacked, after some period of time. She said a black man done attacked her. That ain't so, but that's what she said."

★

Whether it was a Black man that attacked Fannie, or not, it really didn't matter. This was still the Deep South, and when a White woman claimed a Black man assaulted her, a Black man assaulted her.

It didn't matter which Black man, either.

"If he didn't come in on this white lady," argues Edith Foster, "Well, then there'd never been nothing to it."

★

The women sent word up to the mill. Before long, men started arriving.

Fifty-three-year-old Levy County Sheriff Robert Elisha Walker got a phone call from Walter Pillsbury's office. Walter was the former college football star and Spanish-American War adventurer who became mill boss at Cummer Sons. The only phone in town was in his office.

A White woman had been attacked, Pillsbury told the Sheriff. She was saying "it was a negro who did it." He needed to come right away.

The sheriff was twenty miles east at the time, at his office in the county seat, Bronson—barely a crossroads of a town on the Seaboard Railway line—a few houses, some orange trees, B.O. Smith's, which offered groceries, dry goods, hardware and kept funeral caskets upstairs, Carl Wellman's barber shop, the Boyd hotel, a small county courthouse, jail and tax collector's office, a Masonic hall and the Ford dealership.

Bouncing along the craggy limerock road in his Model T Ford, dodging potholes, ruts and a rich canopy of trees trying to reclaim the land, he made it in under an hour.

Walker's twenty-year career in law enforcement took him from the backwater frontier days, when bear hunts and blood feuds were common, to the modern problems of a county overrun with towns and people where only wilderness once stood.

He tried to bring some professionalism to the job. His predecessor, Sheriff H.S. "Cap" Sutton, had been fired quite abruptly after being accused of taking kickbacks, shortchanging the state (it appears he was renting out convicts and $230.47 went missing) and overbilling for the construction of a hanging gallows.

Deputy Sheriff Clarence Williams was there when he arrived. Clarence knew the area well. In addition to his county duties, he was a quarters boss at the mill (a county deputy who doubled as a security guard for a private company). He operated out of Cummer's hotel and boarding house.

A posse had been formed consisting of a dozen men, many in work denims, work shirts, and high-top boots (it was Monday, so most weren't yet caked in mud and tree sap). Some had vests, a few waistcoats. They all wore hats, of course, to guard against the oppressive afternoon sun. A mill manager and foreman arrived in their usual attire: dark pants, starched shirts, ties, long coats, fedoras, and leather shoes. All were armed with pistols or long guns.

Suspicion quickly fell on Jesse Hunter, a Black man serving time on a convict road gang for having carried concealed weapons. He recently escaped a chain gang. Like a lot of pieces to the story, there were other versions. One had him laboring in a turpentine camp, under Florida's notorious convict lease system.

Hunter was reported as having been in the vicinity of Rosewood sometime before the assault. He was allegedly seen in the company of Sam Carter, a forty-five-year-old Black man, and local mason, who previously had been accused of attempting a felony by assaulting a Levy County deputy sheriff with a shotgun.

Sheriff Walker obtained a pack of bloodhounds from Captain H. H. Henderson at Convict Camp Number 17, Fort White, near High Springs in neighboring Alachua County. With all the backwoods and swamps, they'd need them. No telling where Hunter might run to.

★

Jason McElveen, who lived three doors north of the Taylors and was one of the White posse members, told the Sheriff, "Bob, keep them [the posse] out of the colored quarters in the mill [at Sumner] ... We knew if we could keep them N*****s in the mill we could keep them straight, but we knew if we let them out of there the farmers [posse members] would get them."

Walker recognized that if trouble started up at the mill, all hell could break loose. Blacks and Whites working together could be a combustible situation. Walker knew it didn't take much to set people off around these parts.

When Walker first joined the sheriff's office, there was the Lewis case. Brit Lewis and his wife Georgia America Lewis were the wealthiest family in Levy County. Rumor had it that Mr. Lewis kept $20,000 in gold ($1 million today) in a safe in his house.

Tom Faircloth and his best friend, Theo Smith had heard the rumors. The younger Tom was tall and thin with dark hair and a dark mustache. Theo was almost his opposite, shorter and more muscular with sun-bleached hair and a blonde handlebar mustache. Both men were from decent families, but liked to drink and preferred carousing and "hell-raising" to work.

The pair had been farmhands for the Lewis's and were familiar with the property—and not just that, Theo was a distant cousin.

They hatched a plan to break into the safe while the Lewis's were away at dinner—but it all went horribly wrong. The Lewis's were both shot and killed in a gruesome manner and the would-be robbers went on the lam.

News reached Sheriff Walker that Tom Faircloth had been seen purchasing fake mustaches and bullets around the time of the murders.   He was captured at Fort Fanning waiting to make his getaway on the Suwannee River.

Theo had been able to stow away in a rail car headed east. He wouldn't go far, though. As the train passed through Bronson, he stuck his head out to view his hometown that he may never see again. He was spotted. By the time the train got to nearby Archer, Theo was apprehended.

It didn't matter that the two were White, a mob wanted them hung. Walker needed to smuggle the pair out of the jail, which had been surrounded by an ever-increasing crowd of angry citizens calling for a lynching.

He snuck them out right under the noses of the mob who, looking for two White men, never noticed a wagon load of convicts being sent out on lease included two hapless souls in blackface (the men eventually confessed to the murders and were convicted and hung at the Bronson Courthouse).

★

Walker knew his posse was getting restless. He needed to find the man that attacked Fannie Taylor and bring him in before innocent people got hurt.

"I don't know what to do," Deputy Williams said, "this crowd wants blood, and they [are] going to have blood."

"Let's go get 'em, boys," barked Sheriff Walker to the assembled. With that, the hunt was on.

A few pieces of Fannie's clothing were brought out, rubbed on the hounds' noses, and they took off for the backyard, howling and snorting.

★

Into the woods they went, then along the train tracks, a long parade of men stumbling behind the dog handlers.

The dogs were impatient, straining under their leashes. Southern manhunts often followed the railroad, because these offered a fugitive clear direction, unlike roads that looped and wound around the forests and swamps and could get a man lost.

In 1923, Sumner was big enough to have its own barbershop. It had one chair, clippers, and a pool table at the far side of the room. Twenty-three-year-old Marshall Cannon heard a commotion and came out to see what the fuss was all about.

A group of men was rushing out of the scrub over by the tracks, headed in his direction, a pack of hounds in the lead. The butcher, Ed Dorsett, must have heard the noise too, because he came out of the meat market, still in his blood-stained butcher apron. Both Cannon and Dorsett joined in the chase.

As they passed through town, past Dorsett's home, children were pulled inside, doors never locked were bolted, curtains drawn. Those brave enough to peek outside saw a hurried rush of men surge past, many brandishing rifles, shotguns, and dust in the air kicked up by their boots, giving a sallow glow to the light.

★

Leeroy (Lee) Carrier, a 23-year-old Black man from Rosewood, had continued climbing the lumber stacks at the mill, as he usually did, but he kept seeing changes as the day progressed. At mid-morning the whistle blew signaling "quarter-time," then again at noon for lunch, and as the day progressed, he noticed that the White foreman and some of the skilled White craftsman continued to disappear.

Sixteen-year-old Sam Hall noticed something was amiss, too, but he hadn't been at the mill that long. Lumber stacking was a dangerous job. He'd already been injured when he got in the way of a plank being hefted onto the pile—so he didn't give it much mind.

Hall's father, Charles Bacchus Hall, had run the only Black-owned general store in town. It took up the first floor of the family's two-story house. It was in the winter of 1920 when Charles got sick and took to bed. He never got up. He died the next year. The family had to shut down the store. Sam's mother got a job at the mill "dogging" logs—rotating the tree trunks with metal tongs each time the giant saws sliced off a plank.

Back at the hunt, the fugitive seemed close. The dogs were yelping up a storm. Marshall Cannon watched one, as its eager nose did a dance, sniffing along the top of the iron rail, then darting off, only to return to the track. "He's trying to walk that rail!" someone exclaimed.

As Deputy Williams, the dogs, and the pack of pursuers sped northeast along the rail line, they met open country, pastures and clumps of palmetto thicket. Sheriff Walker was following in his Ford. He kept Williams in sight. It was easy. He was wearing a ten-gallon cowboy hat.

Up ahead on the horizon something appeared. It was a rambling one-story house perched near the train tracks. "Hattie," Deputy Williams shouts, "you'all seen any strangers go by?" She shook her head to indicate, "No." It had been rather quiet all day.

This would repeat itself all afternoon as the posse moved east, passing Wylly, where one of the last remaining turpentine camps continued to smoke and boil. There, at one of the shanties belonging to M&M Naval Stores, two White men knocked at the door inquiring about the mysterious stranger, then, without asking, made a quick search and were gone.

★

As the dogs moved eastward they push deeper into civilization, past the First African Methodist Episcopal Church of Rosewood, by the Magnolia Lodge #148, a Masonic hall with the distinction of being for Masons who were Black—"church for the women, lodge for the men."

Some of the buildings were boarded up, abandoned when the Whites left town, some still occupied; then there were the remnants of the long-closed Charpia cedar mill. For decades these red-hearted trees were cut so heedlessly that few now remained.

Onward they pushed, this time on the north side of the tracks, by the railroad freight dock at John Wright's, a White-owned store that the Black residents patronized. Wright was a kind man who passed out candy and cookies to the children.

Up ahead, past the depot and the buildings, a jumble of roof tops appeared. It was Emma Carrier's house, the sister of the washerwoman who saw the White man enter Fannie Taylor's house that morning. The dogs seemed to pay it no mind.

★

"Mama and we all was standing out in the yard and ... here come a gang of crackers, coming down the railroad," notes Minnie, Emma Carrier's granddaughter.

"They was so many...all kinds, horseback, some...riding them little buggy cars down the dirt roads, some of them was in the railroad, just as far as you can see them."

By now the posse had grown to over 100. Falling in behind Sheriff Walker were other vehicles, including one driven by Edward Pillsbury, Walter's son, the mill boss. A turpentine foreman named Jack Cason was on horseback.

Some of the men wore "them big ole' tall hats." Emma was down by the fence, with Minnie clutching her tightly around her skirt. "Emma," one of the men shouts, has anybody been 'long here?" She shook her head "No," and the posse moved on.

Arnett Goins remembered, "They was carrying guns, and they had dogs with them, too."

The posse was getting to the edge of town, almost at the point of leaving Rosewood entirely. Beyond Emma's house was a pungent hermit cabin inhabited by Hardee Davis. He was known to stew up a skunk or two. Past his place were open fields and then the old shanties from an abandoned turpentine camp. It was at the edge of town that all the men in the posse would meet up.

All of the sudden, one of the hounds turned, leaving the tracks, heading back, nose down, determined, pulling its handler along. In minutes they reached the home of a young married couple, Aaron and Gussie (Mahulda) Carrier.

Aaron was Emma's oldest son. He had fought in World War I. It left him jumpy, and he had a heart condition. It didn't stop him from being a "tie cutter," replacing rotted railroad ties. Some claim he used tie-cutting to hide his side business poaching hogs.

Mahulda was the town's schoolteacher. They married during the war.

The bloodhound rushed onto Aaron's porch, then reared and threw its front paws on the door. The men rushed forward, the dog was pulled aside, the door was flung open, the dog sprinted in. No one was home.

Maybe the fugitive had found help. Maybe Carrier aided in his escape. Someone spotted wagon marks in the sand leading to the woods. Is that how he got away?

The posse made a beeline for Emma's house. She answered the pounding on her door to confront a mob of White men. "Where is he?" one shouted. "Where's your boy? We want him. Now!" Emma blocked the doorway. "He's sick," she said. "Sick in bed. He's been sick. He didn't do nothin. What you want him for? He didn't do nothin."

The mob pushed her aside, stormed into the house and found Aaron, up in his mother's bedroom. They dragged him out, ordered him to talk, but he said nothing.

Emma heard one man shout, "Bring a rope!"

Sheriff Walker had to act fast if he was going to contain the situation and maintain any semblance of control. Besides, if he knew something, if he was a conspirator, he could be the key to keeping the manhunt alive. They still needed to find Hunter.

Crying, Emma pleaded, "Please don't hurt him. He didn't do nothin'! He's sick."

Sheriff Walker had a simple face. He was anything but flamboyant. He seemed to make an art out of fading into the background. His gun holster was barely a pouch, worn cross-draw style in front of bunched trousers. He was faced with an ever-more impulsive crowd, challenging his authority. They outnumbered him, so he had to outsmart them.

The crowd tied Aaron to a car and dragged him to an old oak tree on the other side of the tracks, a noose around his neck as he walked. The plan was to haul him up on a low limb, feet just off the ground, and leave him there until he talked.

That's when 53-year-old Jack Cason appeared. His job often made him the lone White man in pine forests worked by crews of Blacks. It was tough work—slashing thousands of tree trunks to bleed out the sticky resin that would go in tar and pitch for wooden ships and turpentine for paints and other use. He was a tough character, like out of the Wild West. He would ride from camp to camp checking and tallying the product.

There was another side to him. Though. Jack had a wife and seven children, and a brother with an adventurous streak: he had divorced and then ran off with Jack's wife's daughter, disappearing into the outlaw swamps beyond the county line, across the big river called the Suwannee.

Stepping out from behind an oak tree, Jack pulled out his pistol and held it up, cocked and fired. In a determined voice he shouted, "Not here, not like this." The crowd turned. No one moved. They knew he was serious. The stocky turpentine woods rider had quite the reputation. Some called him a killer. No one wanted to find out if it was true.

That's all young Ed Pillsbury and his friend Bert Philips needed to distract the mob, as they rescued Aaron with Sheriff Walker and Deputy William's help, tossed him in the back of Pillsbury's car and drove to the jail in Bronson.

Shocked and embarrassed by the ruse, the mob decided to head back to the jail in Sumner to retrieve their prize suspect. After all, the jail was hardly more than a wooden shanty, a holding pen for Saturday night drunks. Little did they know the jail was empty. The Sheriff would have a good laugh about that.

★

The mill whistle blew at exactly 5:45pm, signaling the workday was over. Lee Carrier left the lumber stacks, moving along the railroad tracks in the dusk of evening as he headed back to Rosewood.

Arriving in town, word had finally reached him that something happened to his cousin, Aaron. He headed over to Wright's store.

The atmosphere was different. There were five or six Whites milling around the front. Most knew little why they were there. Some didn't know who Fannie was. It didn't matter. They "knew" a Black boy done messed with a White woman. That's all they needed to know.

As Lee approached the steps to the store, one of the Whites, glared at him. "Well," he said, "we gonna get us a N*****." Then they marched off.

★

A few hours later, with the Sheriff and the Deputy gone, the mob dropped any pretense of lawfulness. It didn't hurt that nighttime was setting in and the moonshine came out. The vigilantes grabbed Samuel S. Carter, as he headed back home on the outskirts of Rosewood.

There wasn't a lot known about the 48-year-old blacksmith and teamster. Some said he was Black. Others said he looked "like an Indian," with his prominent cheekbones and coppery skin. "He looked more like a red Indian," said Pompey Grover, a neighbor from the Otter Creek area, "Just like them big Cherokee Indians ... old long crooked nose." A widower, he lived with his grown daughter on 80 acres, which was originally homesteaded by his father.

He wasn't very friendly. As teenage neighbor Sam Hall remembered, "Sam Carter was mean as a circle saw."

Back in 1900, he had been charged with the attempted murder of Richard Williams, who was married to Carter's sister, Janetta. Carter testified that Williams had shot at him first, then at his sister. He spent a year in jail.

"It was a group of about twenty-five, maybe thirty men, not much of a mob yet. They had been drinkin'. I could smell it," said Ernst Parham. "When I got there they had him stretched out." Parham was excited to be there. He had been kept out of the action all day, trapped in the mill commissary, because its manager, Albert Johnson, pulled rank to run off and join the manhunt.

The mob took Carter to a big tree, tied his hands and feet and hung him with just his toes touching the ground, some in the crowd jeering, some cheering, as he was twisting in the air, boots kicking horribly, writhing, gasping, until at last, "I'll tell you! I'll tell you!" Barely able to speak, he was dropped to the ground, falling into a heap.

He admitted to hitching up his horse and wagon and driving the fugitive away (presumably back toward Rosewood). Carter said he would lead the posse to a spot where he and the fugitive parted ways.

They proceeded on foot, like a conga line dancing along, composed of every White male curious to witness the show. By now there were hundreds. They moved deeper and deeper into the Gulf Hammock. They were about to break the case wide open. And they were thirsty for blood. "N***** blood."

When they reached the spot, Carter told them, "Here's where I put him out." But the dogs didn't smell anything. There was no scent to follow. The torture resumed.

As an eyewitness recalled, "So, he wouldn't tell 'em, so they say if you don't tell them, we gonna kill you, he say well you can kill me, but he said you can't eat me! So they hung 'em up, they killed him and shot holes in him."

Some in the mob took souvenirs of his clothes. "They done took his fingers and his ears. That was the type of people they was."

"My cousin Bryant kilt that N*****," exclaimed Perry Hudson. At twenty-three years old, Bryant Hudson already had a reputation as a destitute alcoholic and petty thief. He and his brother, David, were tried for attempting to kill a sheriff with a knife, but the two were let off.

"Let's kill the son of a bitch," Sumner barber Marshall Cannon recalled Bryant saying. And then he did. With the smell of cheap cane liquor on his breath and a shotgun in his hands, he leveled the weapon and pulled the trigger. Sam Carter's face was blown off. "He killed the N*****, killed the evidence."

"Oh, my God. Now we'll never know," exclaimed Walter Pillsbury when he heard.

"He knew nothin' about nothin'," said Robie Mortin, one of the Black children from Rosewood. "He was comin' home from his job at the turpentine still, knowin' nothin' about nothin' and he was tortured and lynched and hung. They left him there all day and night."

Someone grabbed Carter's pocket watch. From time to time, in a bar, in the barbershop, around Sumner or Cedar Keys, someone would say, "Let's see what time it is by ol' Sam Carter," and the watch would come out.

One boy who saw the watch would grow up to become a Florida legislator, Randolph Hodges, who was part of the Pork Chop Gang, a group of Democratic Party legislators who worked together to dominate the Florida legislature, especially to maintain segregation and conserve the disproportionate political power of mostly rural northern Florida.

The next morning a coroner's jury was called on to review Carter's death. Justice of the Peace, L.L. Johns, a former sawmill security guard, would hold court in Drew Pearson's drug store. The six-man panel issued its report the same day: "We the Jury after the examination of the said Sam Carter who being found lying dead, find that the said Sam Carter came to his death by being shot by unknown party [or parties] so say we all."

★

As the manhunt continued on Tuesday. Jason McElveen, who ran a "motorcar" (a gasoline-powered cart that ran on the train tracks) for the mill, drove to Otter Creek, 12 miles up from Rosewood to pick up two more blood-hounds from Fort White.

Now that the posse was without its star witnesses—Aaron Carrier and Sam Carter—Emma Carrier started getting this uneasy feeling her family was next. Maybe they should get out of sight?

Her oldest daughter, Beulah Carrier (everyone called her Scrappy), lived and worked in Wylly's jook joint at the turpentine camp. She had married Frank Sherman, a handsome preacher, but the marriage lasted only three years.

At the time, alcohol sale and consumption were illegal under both state and federal laws, so "jook joints" were popular throughout the area. Many operated in shanties and old barns. They featured moonshine, dancing and gambling.

A jook joint's back room offered a card game called Georgia Skin, "a kind of lethal blackjack, able to create a pauper or a prince at a stroke—attracting a stream of questionable gamblers and card cheats, some with fancy clothes and jewelry, some with cardboard suitcases and a smile.

Every Saturday night, the jook joint at Wylly "brought in a (train) carload of colored ladies from points north, some as far away as Jacksonville," notes one of the supervisors at the turpentine camp. "By midnight the joint was jumpin'. It usually closed in the wee hours with a fusillade that reminded one of the trenches of World War I, leaving the roof with a swiss cheese appearance due to bullet holes from many weekend brawls."

Why not have the family stay with her, said Scrappy. Emma, who banned any sort of dancing in her house, was aghast. If Scrappy wants to live in a den of iniquity, that's her choice, but there was no way she would set foot in that place and certainly not the children—regardless of the dangers at home!

It's the devil's house!

★

Tuesday and Wednesday were rather uneventful, spent mostly in a fruitless search for the elusive fugitive Jesse Hunter. Some returned to their jobs at the mill, others drifted into the backwoods and beyond. Then on Thursday, January 4, violence broke out on a large scale.

Early that evening reports came in that a group of Blacks had taken refuge in a Rosewood home. No one believed that Hunter was among them, but a "party of citizens" decided to "investigate." They were particularly interested in locating Sylvester Carrier, Sarah's son.

He had a spirited manner, like in how he dressed. Sometimes, to emphasize his dark complexion he would wear white shirts and white Stetson hats. Often, though, he preferred all black—black suit, black tie, black Stetson.

Sylvester had past troubles with the law. Both Sylvester and his father Haywood spent the summer of 1918 working on one of the state's notoriously brutal road gangs for "animal mark changing," which, simply put, meant they were stealing hogs off neighboring properties.

He had a softer side, too. Married to Gertrude for ten years, he lived in his mother Sarah's house and gave lessons on the mail-order piano to earn extra money. When he wasn't working, he was usually out hunting. Sylvester kept three dogs in a pen out in back of the house. He had a deer dog he called Rattler, a bird dog named Kate, and a rabbit dog named Trixie. He'd usually come back with as many gophers, flushed from the holes where the rabbits liked to hide—but it didn't matter. They were all good eating, with the rabbits parboiled and then fried, just like chicken. The gophers were usually simmered and stewed, like beef.

While bigger than life in the Black community, Sylvester was unpopular with certain Whites. He was proud, too proud, not in fear of White men. "They felt he was all *uppity*." He had supposedly remarked that the assault on Fannie Taylor was "an example of what [Negroes] could do without interference."

The Whites planned to warn Carrier against further incendiary talk and to discover what he or the others knew about Hunter. One of the posse remarked that Sylvester's high-and-mighty talk, "was just about like throwing gasoline on a fire when you tell a bunch of white people that."

But that's the kind of person he was. Sylvester Carrier was someone who went about his business, "he didn't bother nobody, he didn't want nobody bothering with him or his people."

He didn't like for those Black girls in town to go walking up the road to Sumner with the White guys, "you know to throw WOLF cracks at girls," says one of his friends, "you know, and so he didn't wait to tomorrow or a week later to see this person who be sayin' that. He go right to their house & tell 'em, walk right into their yard and tell 'em, 'don't you be doin' that.'"

"At that same time, we could not even look at a white woman. A black man couldn't look at a white woman even if they were just standing up and be thinking about it. If the whites feel that a black man was doing that, they would kill him or beat him up."

Lee Carrier remembers seeing Sylvester early that bright moonlit Thursday night. He looked drained. "They said they were comin' Monday; they didn't come Monday. They say they was comin' Tuesday; they didn't come Tuesday. They said they was comin' Wednesday; they didn't come … Syl sent 'em word he was at home and he hadn't bothered nobody. Come on."

One of the local Whites put in more succinctly: "This N***** sent 'em word: Come and get him."

★

Henry Andrews was a 42-year-old "wood boss," or superintendent, of the Cummer Lumber Company's sawmill. He was short, but stocky and powerful. He was known for his quick temper and his habit of kicking workers when they moved to slow for his liking. "Boots" they called him.

"Kick 'em?" said Sam Hall, "White of black. He wasn't playin' bad. He was bad."

"He didn't just beat up colored, "said Robert Missouri, who worked a Cummer in the shingle mill, "He beat up white, too."

Forty-five-year-old, ruddy-faced "Poly" Wilkerson, an ex-deputy sheriff and ex-quarters boss, the father of five, still acting as a constable, was a "big, blustery fellow" who weighed well over two hundred pounds. Black or White, he cared for few people, and fewer still cared for him.

Weary of complaints from workers about Wilkerson's heavy hand, the mill management had recently fired him. Wilkerson didn't take the dismissal well. One evening, he challenged his replacement, Clarence Williams (who also became the county deputy), to a gun fight, but Williams beat him to the draw. "Well, now," Williams exclaimed, "You pull your trigger and I'll pull mine." With that, Wilkerson backed down.

Hearing about the troubles in Rosewood, Henry Andrews headed down from Otter Creek in a railroad motorcar full of armed men. Wilkerson filled his Model T with a few friends and drove up. The two groups collected in front of the Carrier house.

These two firebrands would stoke the fires of hatred and lead a mob just itching to kill some Blacks.

"There were quite a few men around that building," remembered Willard Hathcox, who was part of the original posse. "They was shooting, upstairs, downstairs, everywhere there was moving they was shootin. That's when my uncle, Poly Wilkerson, stepped up."

"He shouted into the house, 'Syl, come out. We ain't playin' games. You better get your ass out here, or we're coming in,'" remembers Arnett Goins who was eight at the time. He was hiding in one of the upstairs bedrooms with the other children.

Wilkerson drew his pistol and shot a yapping puppy the children called Shant Tail who was tied up next to the porch. Killed it dead.

"The first to kill was the dog. They shot my dog!" said Minnie.

"Yep, Poly done shot that dog, yessir," said Jason McElveen.

As Andrews and Wilkerson approached the front porch, Sarah walked to the front of the hallway and hollered out, "Ya'all go on home!," almost scolding them like they were children—some she had helped raise. "Just get yourselves on home," she added.

Wilkerson fired off one shot striking Sarah, then rushed the front door with Andrews hot on his heels. Before they made it into the house Sylvester returned fire with a Winchester Model 12-gauge repeating shotgun.

BOOM!

Sylvester squeezed the trigger with a deafening blast. Then again. BOOM!

The two White men fell dead where they stood.

"He was poppin' everyone he saw," said one of the children in the house. "If they come through that door, he done kilt them."

"He was the onliest one that would fight," said Lonnie Carrol (Carrier).

"And the next one jump up there, and Sly shot him, too," said Minnie Langley, one of the children hiding upstairs. "They kept a'comin' and he was knockin' 'em down."

Andrews and Wilkerson were the second and third persons to be killed since Monday.

★

"Aunt Sarah said, 'y'all better come on up here to mama house because these crackers look like they gonna raise sand up here,'" notes Minnie. "They gonna come back here and try to kill us tonight.' We stayed to Aunt Sarah's house that night, because ah-and sure enough—mama had told us to go on upstairs and go to bed. We had done went upstairs and got off all our clothes and got in the bed, and that night them crackers came back in there shooting."

Arnett recalls how all the kids were horse playing and staying awake though they were supposed to get to sleep, when the gun shots rang out and all hell broke loose. The children dove to the floor, bullets flying through the windows—but the first thing Arnett thought about was the brand new suit his parents got him for Christmas. All he could think about was to get downstairs and find his suit, which he did as soon as the shooting stopped.

In the commotion, no one noticed 13-year-old Ruben Mitchell, who had been lying in bed but jerked up when the shooting began, got hit with three pellets. One of the other children found a towel to soak up the blood. Ruben was frozen with panic. The wound was not fatal, but he lost his left eye.

Minnie Carrier recalls Bernadina (who they called "Honey) run upstairs with blood all over her nightgown, and "she told us that mama got killed, that mama was dead." Being barefoot, she remembered the stairs being cold "I come on downstairs and I was trembling, cause I was looking for mama. I was looking in there to see if I can see mama. They done shot mama!"

Sarah Carrier would become the fourth victim.

As described by the *Jacksonville Times-Union*, they began "to pour a hail of lead into it." From inside their fire was returned. Most came from Sylvester Carrier. Four more White men were wounded.

Cephus "Sephis" Studstill, a 23-year-old lumber inspector foreman from Cummers and 30-year-old Bryan Kirkland a woodland farmer, were both shot in the arm. Henry Odum of Jacksonville who worked at Otter Creek, a settlement on the railroad a few miles north of Rosewood, was also wounded.

The fourth man, Manny Hudson, a 27-year-old woodland farmer from nearby Janney, who joined in because he was drunk and wanted to have some fun, sustained a scalp wound. "He was just a regular reprobate, drunk," said Jim Turner, a physician at Cummers and Seaboard Air Line Railway, "working just a day here and then … just a tough drunk." Manny refrained from groaning as he lay on that cold floor, "fearing to alert the army of black savages thought to be in the house."

The *Washington Post* reported, "…the negro and a number of his friends had barricaded themselves in a shanty on the outskirts of the town and defied any white man to come near them." The paper accused Sylvester of being a "negro desperado," who was practically waging a one-man "RACE WAR," as though he was a rebellious Nat Turner looking to kill all Whites.

"NEGROES FIRED FIRST," reported the Ocala Florida *Evening Star*, adding, "PLENTY NEGROES IN PARTY."

★

It was late [Thursday night]," says Parham, "probably close to about ten o'clock. It couldn't have been after that because the electricity was always cut off at ten. The hotel [in Sumner] was one of the few places in town with electric lights … We were sittin' in a circle around the living room fireplace, there by the lobby. Clarence Williams came up and took a seat.

"The fire was poppin' and cracklin' like it would, and ol' Clarence sat down and said, 'All hell is takin' place up in Rosewood.' He said something about a group getting' set to go up to Sylvester Carrier's home.

"And it wasn't much after that the lights were still on, and in comes one of the fellas that was stayin' in the hotel, and he had four bullet wounds through his arm. He was all banged up. He didn't stand 'round and talk too much. He was headed up to his room. But he say some men killed over in Rosewood."

"Lots of unfamiliar faces, people I'd never seen before, coming in and asking for shells and guns. We sold to them that could pay. Sold a lot."

"You ain't never seen a mob like that," said a then 15-year-old Fred Kirkland, who witnessed the scene. "They went wild. They was a thousand to fifteen hundred people by that time, and they comin' in from every direction. And they gave that sheriff and deputy five minutes to get out of sight and not come back …

and they left there, and they went to burnin' houses and killin' people like you've never seen."

★

Acting on requests from Sheriff Walker and town officials, Alachua County's Sheriff P. G. Ramsey was requested to start immediately for Rosewood with as many men as he could assemble.

By one o'clock on Friday morning Sheriff Ramsey, Chief Deputy Dunning, and several carloads of deputies and armed citizens were preparing to leave for Levy County.

Among those coming from Gainesville were several members of the Ku Klux Klan, who had held a major rally in town that Monday. A large crowd, including some Northern tourists, watched as an estimated one hundred Klansmen in full regalia paraded through downtown Gainesville.

The white-clad figures carried banners proclaiming their opposition to boot-leggers, gamblers, and cheating lawyers. One placard declared, "First And Al-ways--Protect Womanhood."

At Rosewood the battle was still in progress at 2:30 Friday morning. One news-paper reported White authorities as believing that unless the Blacks surrendered "they will be smoked out."

At some point one of the attackers, armed with a flashlight, worked his way across the open space between the crowd and the house. He climbed through a darkened window and switched on his flashlight. He was quickly shot, then fell back through the window onto the ground.

There were no further attempts to enter the house. The Blacks seemed well supplied with arms and ammunition, and the bright moonlight made the attackers such easy targets that they contented themselves with a siege. Desultory firing from a safe distance ceased around 4:00am, when the Whites' ammunition ran low. More shells and bullets were ordered from Gainesville, as they waited for daylight before making another move and to tend to the wounded.

Many in the bullet-riddled house were able to use the ceasefire to make good their escape. Sophie (Goins) and John Monroe were hiding out in the house. They fled into the nearby woods and swamps—some in little more than their nightshirts—and were joined by the other Blacks in Rosewood who feared that they would also be attacked.

"We walked through water," said Lee Ruth, "we sat on a log on that trail … the log was laying deep in the water … we sat there and just begged to go home."

"In January, it ain't too hot, and we got everyone out of bed at the spur of the moment with nutin' on, nutin' to wear, no food or nutin' to get in them woods," recalled then seven-year-old Wilson Hall, "we could hear guns shootin' from a distance, you know, they ain't huntin' rabbits and squirrels. They huntin' people—and here we is, sittin' here like sittin' ducks, and the onlyist protection we got is the woods and what god provided for us."

Scrappy Carrier heard about the trouble and came to get the children. "There was a pile of them," she noted.

"It was cold, man, it was cold. Jesus, I will never forget that day," said one of the children that escaped. "It was so cold, but Beulah (Scrappy) wouldn't let us build but a little bitty fire."

★

State newspapers—many with a racist slant—reported the events at Rosewood in bold headlines and some took large liberties in describing what was happening. According to the *Miami Daily Metropolis*, which headlined its story, MANY DIE IN FLORIDA RACE WAR, "Deputized posses and citizens said to be numbering in the thousands were pouring into this village early this morning."

Black newspapers covered the events from a different angle. *The Afro-American* in Baltimore highlighted the acts of Black heroism against the onslaught of "savages." Another newspaper reported: "Two Negro women were attacked and raped between Rosewood and Sumner. The sexual lust of the brutal white mobbists satisfied, the women were strangled."

Early on Friday the bodies of Andrews and Wilkerson were retrieved so preparations could be made for their respective burials. Frances Smith, who had been at Fannie's side when this whole mess started, remembered Wilkerson's funeral oration at Shiloh Cemetery, of the preacher, an unshaven circuit rider adorned in a shallow-tail coat, white high-collar shirt, string tie and a black wide-brimmed hat, who happened to be in Sumner for a tent revival—shouted over the grave with such passion and force that a steady torrent of brown-stained tobacco juice rained down onto the coffin.

★

On entering the house, there were the body of Sylvester Carrier alongside that of his mother Sarah Carrier. The death toll had now risen to five.

Thwarted by the escape and angered by the deaths of two Whites and the wounding of several others, the "infuriated" mob quickly "tore down pictures, smashed furniture, and completely ransacked the black dwelling."

"They even took the chickens," said Lee Ruth ("Mossy") Davis, Sylvester's niece, "and then were runnin' down the screaming pigs."

It is unknown what attempts Sheriff Walker made to stop the Whites or what assistance Sheriff Ramsey was able to render. In any case, the mob burned the Carrier home so that "nothing but ashes was left to tell the tale of the gun fight."

They next burned five more houses and a church in the Black section. "Poured kerosene on and lit it up," said one observer.

★

Lexie Gordon, a 50-year-old light-skinned Black woman with fiery red hair, ill with "typhoid-malaria fever" (a non-cerebral strain common at the time to Florida), who had sent her children into the woods, heard the men on her front porch. Racked with pain, chills and fever, she managed to pull herself up out of bed. When smoke started curling through her front window, Lexi attempted to flee out the back.

"When they set the house on fire," notes Edith Foster, who lived across the street, "well she done ran out towards the back, and she had a back door johnny, you know, out there, and she made for it, and they shot her before she got there."

Silhouetted by the flames in the background, she was an easy target. She was killed with the single shotgun blast to her face. Lexie became the sixth victim.

Lee Ruth Davis heard the bells tolling in the church as the men were inside setting it on fire. Even the White church in Rosewood was destroyed.

Mary Hall had four daughters and five sons. "All of us children were in bed and my mother was gone to bed," says a daughter, Marge. "She came into our room and woke us up and said, 'Y'all get up, they're shooting.' We didn't have time to put any clothes on. We just jumped up and ran out the house and took off into the woods going (the 15 miles) toward Wylly."

Friday night, Walter Pillsbury burst into the Sumner hotel lobby. "We got to stop this mob," he said. "They are comin' this way."

"He said he wanted as many of us as had guns to come with him," said Parham. "Well, every one of us had guns. You carried a pistol from the time you was fifteen … It was a cold night. Gosh it was cold. We all went out to the edge of town, the east end, closest to Rosewood. They was a spur at the railroad track there, and we lined up across the road right at the spur, about twenty of us."

They didn't wait long. The electric streetlamps casting harsh shadows of a something ahead moving towards them.

"We could hear 'em coming. They were talkin' loud. You could tell they'd been drinkin'. It was dark, about nine-thirty. Mister Pillsbury had us line up from one side of the road to the other, and then they come up that spur, about a hundred feet away from us, he called out to them, told them that the first man set foot on that rail, he would personally shoot him. He said he had orders to shoot anybody that came across that track. Well, that stopped them … They turned and went back."

Although most Whites sided with the mob, there were a few examples of Whites who aided the Black residents. Some Black women and children escaped the woods and swamps thanks to John and William Bryce, two Northerners who had come south to run a railroad. Aware of the violence in Rosewood, the brothers drove their train to the area and offered to help people escape.

"Captain Bryce, he was so good to us," said one of the children. "You know, everybody was hollerin' and cryin' and prayin', and they put us all on the train."

In Sumner, Ernest Parham's mother and stepfather, a man named Markham, smuggled their cook, Liza Bradley, out of town—hidden under laundry in the back seat of a car and driven past the roadblock. A few of Sumner's White women hid Black women and children and later helped them escape.

In Rosewood, John Wright and his wife, Mary, hid a bunch of Black women and children. As the mob approached the house, Mary leveled a shotgun, looked them in the eye and said she'd kill the first man to take a step through the gate. The men moved on. The next day, when the train pulled up at the railroad platform in back of his store, John Wright quickly loaded the survivors into the darkened cars where they were spirited away to Gainesville.

★

On Friday afternoon a seventh death occurred.

Mingo Williams was a Black turpentine worker whose nickname was Lord God—a name his mother gave him when he was a baby. Now he was 50 years old and living in a small cabin by the woods, making a living by "scraping," where the resin inside the pines grew thick and unworkable in the winter months, the crust could be flaked off and sold.

That's where Mingo was, just shy of Bronson, a slight slope descends from into imposing flatwoods, where the road meets the coastal lowlands, when a car filled with White men pulled up beside him.

"What's your name, boy?" they asked.

"Lord God," he replied.

A rifle was raised, a blast from its barrel, and he was shot through the jaw. His body was found on the road near Bronson. Williams had no known connection with the trouble at Rosewood.

★

By nightfall, Sheriff Walker told the Associated Press that more trouble was imminent because relatives of the slain Blacks were believed to be armed and were expected to cause trouble, although most were hiding in the woods fearful of their lives.

Meanwhile, Ramsey and his deputies had returned to Gainesville on Friday afternoon because they believed local officers had matters under "fairly good control."

Learning about the turbulent conditions at Rosewood from the dispatches, Governor Cary Hardee, the former high school principal in neighboring Perry Florida, sent a telegram to the sheriff asking for a situation report. Throughout the day the governor waited for a reply. When he didn't hear back, that afternoon he felt comfortable enough to go turkey hunting.

Late in the afternoon a telegram arrived. The sheriff briefly told the governor that local authorities had the situation under control. There was no need to activate the national guard. As events turned out, the situation was far from under control, but the governor accepted the opinion of the Levy County sheriff and never sent troops.

That same day (Friday) a Black man answering the physical description of Hunter was arrested in Lakeland, about 130 miles south of Rosewood. Two deputies and two citizens of Rosewood who knew Hunter went to Lakeland. Although the prisoner closely resembled the fugitive, he was not Hunter. The search continued.

★

James Carrier, brother of Sylvester and son of Sarah, was one of the besieged occupants who escaped. On Saturday morning he left his hideout in a nearby swamp and returned to Rosewood.

There he asked Walter Pillsbury, the White superintendent of the Cummer mill, for protection. Pillsbury, with his strict Baptist piety, obliged and locked Carrier in one of the remaining houses in Rosewood's Black section. Later in the day, as the *Jacksonville Times-Union* put it, "when a new clash became imminent, the negro was turned over to ... twenty-five or thirty men."

Carrier was taken to the Black graveyard. There beside the fresh graves of his mother and brother, he was "interrogated."

James was not one to back down. His son, Lonnie, recalled how his father would go on all-night hunts in the woods, returning with a deer slung over his shoulder, his shot sack stuffed with small game. One time, Lonnie remembers, James watched as a wounded deer ran out of the woods and tangled in the fence before his father killed it. A White man appeared and shouted that the deer was rightfully his, because he shot it first. But James menacingly leveled a shotgun and the horseman galloped away.

His inquisitors demanded the names of the people in the house who had participated in the shooting. They especially wanted to know if Jesse Hunter was one of them. Carrier admitted that he had been in the house but escaped, yet he refused to name the others. His captors then shot him several times. The body count now numbered eight.

"They killed my granddaddy," recalled Minnie Lee Langley. "Made him dug his own hole, he didn't have but one arm (from a debilitating stroke), but they made him dug his own grave, and he prayed and they shot him backwards in the grave."

★

Most Black residents of Rosewood remained in hiding in the woods and swamps, and Blacks in Sumner and other villages did not dare venture from their quarters. "We could see the white people in their trucks with their guns sticking up on the trucks and cars right behind them, said one frightened resident. "This went on all day and all night. We could see where they were burning the houses ... We could see the balls of black smoke."

"And they was killin' everything breathin'," exclaimed Lee Ruth Davis. "if you was black. Just like they was huntin'."

At Sumner, all Blacks who were not at work in the lumber mill were kept in the quarters, and a "dead line" was established between the Black and White sections, and a curfew made effective.

Following the wholesale burning of buildings on Friday morning, only twelve Black houses were left in Rosewood. On Sunday afternoon a crowd of Whites, estimated at 100-150, gathered and watched as the remaining houses were torched, one by one.

"They just a bad crew that come in here," remembered Edith Foster, "and they wiped it to the map."

"We was seein' things on fire," said Minnie Langley. "just burnin' up the whole thing, just burnin' up my grandmama house, churches and everything, everything we had, all our clothes and everything. They burn it up. They was mad."

The AP report declared, "The burning of the houses was carried out deliberately, and, although the crowd was present all the time, no one could be found who would say he saw the houses fired."

"Masses of twisted steel were all that remained of furniture formerly in the negro homes, [and] several charred bodies of dogs, and firearms left in the hasty retreat, bore evidence to the mob's fury which set fire to the negro section of [Rosewood]....," reported the *Norfolk Journal and Guide*.

Although Hunter remained at large, officers believed they finally had the situation under control.

There was no one left to kill. The crowd faded away as quickly as it appeared.

By Monday, January 9, the *Times-Union* had relegated the story to page seven.

Walter F. White, a Black activist and authority on lynching who later would become Executive Secretary of the NAACP, sent a letter to a New York newspaper about the deaths of the Blacks at Rosewood. "Their crime was that their skins were black." White reduced the issue to a single query: "Let us put aside any considerations of humanity or decency—the American conscience is no longer shocked by murders at home. The question to be faced is simply this: How long can America get away with it?"

★

A true number of dead in Rosewood was never determined. Jason McElveen, a White man who participated in the affair and was rumored to have ties to the Ku Klux Klan, had a memory that challenged contemporary reports.

He claimed that after the Thursday battle, "they went up there and buried seventeen N*****s out of the house. And I don't know how many more that they picked out of the woods and the fields about the area.

"They just took 'em and laid out in the road [and] plowed the furrows, with a big field-plow, extra big field-plow, fire plow. [They] plowed two big furrows there and put them N*****s in there in the trench and plowed it over.

"There is no markings or anything; don't know who they was, why they was, and they said there was twenty-six of them there."

James Turner, 11 years old at the time, who would later become sheriff of the county, reached Rosewood with his father—the railroad and mill company doctor—by motorcar just as the smoke was clearing from the burning buildings. They were directed to a clearing by a stand of trees.

"It was a hole ... looked like it was dug with shovels," he said. "It was filled with corpses. They said there was 18 of them—corpses of blacks. I couldn't count them ... the way they was thrown in there.

He vividly remembered the diapers. "There were little children ... six months old. Shot."

★

CHAPTER FIVE
AFTERMATH

"History, despite its wrenching pain, Cannot be unlived, but if faced With courage, need not be lived again."

—MAYO ANGELOU, *On The Pulse of Morning*

Days after the Rosewood riot, Governor Hardee appointed a special grand jury and special prosecuting attorney to investigate the outbreak in Rosewood and other incidents in Levy County.

Augustus V. Long, who had a fondness for bow ties and a reputation for fairness and impartiality, was the sitting judge of the Eighth Judicial Circuit.

George DeCottes, a forty-three-year-old World War I veteran and prosecuting attorney for the Seventh Judicial Circuit, replaced A. S. Crews, the regular state attorney for the eighth district, possibly because he had failed to secure a conviction in a recent lynching in Newberry.

The pair were charged with inquiring into "certain high crimes that have been committed by unidentified parties or persons."

In February 1923, the all-White grand jury composed of farmers and merchants was empaneled in Bronson. Before a packed courtroom, Judge Long instructed the jurors to make every effort to fix the blame where it belonged and to see that the "guilty parties are brought to justice."

On February 13th, thirteen witnesses testified. At the end of that first day, DeCottes declined to comment on whether sufficient evidence had been obtained to secure indictments. The prosecuting attorney explained that he could not discuss the matter but said that the incident was being thoroughly investigated.

The next day, examination of witnesses—25 Whites and 8 Blacks, that were scheduled to testify—ended shortly before noon so that DeCottes could go to Gainesville and subpoena more witnesses.

After another full day of testimony, grand jury's foreman, R. C. Philpett, a prominent Levy County farmer, reported that the jurors regretted being unable to find evidence on which to base any indictments. No one would be charged.

A few editorials appeared in Florida newspapers summarizing the event. The *Gainesville Daily Sun* (which openly supported the Ku Klux Klan) justified the actions of Whites involved, writing "Let it be understood now and forever that he, whether white or black, who brutally assaults an innocent and helpless woman, shall die the death of a dog."

The *Tampa Tribune,* in a rare comment on the excesses of Whites in the area, called it "a foul and lasting blot on the people of Levy County."

"They all went to Bronson," noted Bertie Bryant, a local resident. "Nobody knew anything. They weren't goin' tell nothin."

"That's the way it was back then," observed another local, W. Baylor. "They all had a bunch of kinfolks and you couldn't convict all of 'em. Somethin' could happen to you."

★

When the Florida state legislation ended convict leasing in 1919, at the same time, it passed a law empowering employers—including turpentine operators—to hold workers liable for "debt." If an individual accepted a consideration of value-such as transportation to the camp of the employer, under those circumstances, his subsequent failure to perform "shall be prima facie evidence of the intent to injure and defraud."

A few months after the Rosewood Massacre, Florida's abusive system of peonage (the use of laborers bound in servitude because of debt) gained national attention. It came about following an incident involving a 22-year-old White farmworker from North Dakota, Martin Tabert, who was arrested in Tallahassee, Florida on a charge of vagrancy for being on a train without an 80¢ ticket.

Tabert was convicted and fined $25. Although his parents sent money to pay the fine, plus $25 for Tabert to return home, the money disappeared in the Leon County prison system where Sheriff James Robert Jones earned $15 for every prisoner he leased out (and the state earned $35 per able-bodied prisoner per month). In the prior four months, Jones had delivered 163 prisoners to the work camp.

According to a witness, Thomas Walter Higginbotham, the chief whipping boss at a turpentine camp in Dixie County owned by the Putnam Lumber Company, "whipped Martin about thirty-five to fifty licks" with a 5-foot-long leather strap, and when Martin didn't stand up, this angered Higginbotham further and he said, "haven't you had enough?" propped him up and started whipping Tabert again.

Several prisoners reported that when they got Tabert in the sleeping shack and removed his clothes his "skin was all off his back in one chunk from his shoulders to his knees." Tabert died five days later.

It was not clear what he had done to enrage Higginbotham, but one report suggested that Tabert had complained about his prison-issued shoes.

A lumber company letter to the family listed the cause of death as "complication of diseases," and charged the family $20 for the return of the body.

Higginbotham's lawyer argued that the Putnam Lumber Company employed him to discipline the prisoners and he had not broken any law because corporal punishment was legal in Florida. Higginbotham would be convicted of second-degree murder and given a 20-year prison sentence, however, it would be overturned on appeal.

Higginbotham immediately returned to work at the camp. Months later, Lewis "Peanut" Barker, a Black turpentine worker, was beaten and shot to death near Shamrock. One of the accused was Higginbotham, but the case never made it to court.

Sheriff Jones was removed from office, but he was not otherwise punished—although legislative investigators found evidence that he was arresting persons on vagrancy charges solely to fulfill an agreement he had with the Putnam Lumber Company to furnish it with workers.

Florida Governor Cary Hardee at first dismissed the incident as an isolated case, but investigations of the Tabert killing led to evidence of widespread abuses and found that peonage was standard practice at the Baker County turpentine camps belonging to State Senator T. J. Knabb and his brothers.

Through cunning, intelligence and an absolute iron fist, the Knabbs built one of the largest turpentine empires in the country, and owned over 200,000 acres of pine forest in Baker County, which comprised half the county.

Twenty-one laborers died in Knabb's camp in the year leading up to the investigation. A prison inspector who visited one of the camps described it as "a human slaughter pen." A social worker, Thelma Franklin, testified that the warden of the Knabb camp had shot and killed Mary Sheffield, a Black woman, days before she was to have appeared before the committee as a material witness against the Knabbs.

The state legislature's investigation charged that there were as many as 400 Black convicts who worked in Knabb's turpentine distillery and lived in squalid huts, and were being kept by perpetual debt (workers received from fifty cents to a dollar a day and forced to buy provisions at a commissary that charged prices twice those of stores in the area) and a guard system in his employ. All roads leading from "the quarters" were watched closely, and no one was permitted to leave. Beatings were administered frequently.

Some of Knabb's colleagues tried to have him removed from the senate because of the revelations, but nothing came of it or the investigation. In fact, Knabb was allowed to continue leasing prisoners—based on his word that conditions would be improved.

To protect workers, an anonymous group of businessmen in Macclenny Florida (home of Knabb Turpentine) took up a collection and paid the fines owed by the convicts held at the Knabb camp. Three days later, a fire destroyed most of the Macclenny business district, and the Hotel Macclenny burnt to the ground.

In 1936, the U.S. solicitor general announced that the Justice Department was again looking into Knabb Turpentine employment practices, citing numerous complaints of involuntary servitude and peonage. In November of that year, the Knabbs and two others were charged with violations of peonage laws. They pleaded not guilty and were released on bonds of one thousand dollars each. Although the prosecution proved that the chief witness for the defense at the trial had perjured himself, Knabb and his co-defendants were acquitted.

★

Some might say that the Rosewood Massacre was "whitecapping"—the use by Whites of terrorism, torture, fear and intimidation to drive Blacks off their land.

All it took was the cry of "rape" or some other false charge, and if they weren't killed, many times Blacks fled for their lives—only to have their abandoned property seized or acquired for pennies on the dollar.

The timing seemed right. After all, by 1923, the first ripples of the Florida real estate boom were appearing, even in the backwoods of Levy Country.

The state of Florida had even budgeted the then-astronomical sum of $100,000 to build a paved highway, Highway 24—cutting right through Rosewood and Sumner—out to Cedar Key, that began construction that fateful New Year's day of 1923.

Boston swindler Charles Ponzi, operating under the alias of Charles Borelli, moved down to Jacksonville Florida not long after, bought 100 acres and started selling lots at $10 a piece. Within a few weeks, Ponzi had collected $7,000 from hapless investors before state officials shut down his operation and arrested him for failing to file proper papers and selling certificates of indebtedness without permission. Ponzi escaped from jail and a nationwide manhunt began.

He made it to Tampa and under the alias of Andrea Luciana, signed aboard as a waiter and dishwasher on a freighter bound for Italy. Ponzi had disguised himself by growing a mustache and shaving his head. The ruse fooled no one. He was quickly recognized and returned to the U.S., where he served a year of hard labor at the Florida State Penitentiary in Raiford.

A few short years later, the real estate boom was over, its fate sealed by the great hurricane of 1926 (hundreds were killed and 43,000 left homeless as a 15-foot wall of water rolled over eastern coastal cities moving at 150 miles an hour). Ponzi's scheming didn't turn out much better. He eventually found his way to Brazil, where he died in a charity hospital in Rio de Janeiro in 1949 (leaving $75 to pay for his own burial).

If there were any thoughts of appropriating the properties of Rosewood's Black families to cash in on the real estate bonanza, they went up in smoke just like the town had.

★

A year after the Rosewood Massacre, Sheriff Walker ran for election against L. L. (Lottie Luconie—which is why he preferred just initials) Johns, who, a year earlier had presided over the inquest into the death of Sam Carter. L.L. Johns was a colorful character. He favored cowboy boots and tremendous western cowboy hats along with two guns in fast-draw holsters. After 22 years of serving the public Walker found himself out of a job. He said that the people had indicated that they no longer wanted him so he would get out of the way right then. Robert Elisha "Bob" Walker died in 1945 at the age of 76.

At the request of Cummer Sons Cypress, James and Fannie Taylor moved to another mill town near Jacksonville. It was said she was "very nervous" in her later years. Fannie succumbed to cancer in 1965 at the age of 65. Henry James Taylor died in 1972 at the age of 78.

The Taylors would have a third son in 1929, Kenneth James Taylor. He would be the first of the siblings to die, in 1986 at the age of 56. Addis Donald Taylor passed away in 1995 at the age of 72, and his brother Berness "Barney" Gray Taylor died in 2007 at the age of 88.

Aaron Carrier was held in jail for several months, then released. Fearful of reprisals, he and his wife, Mahulda, changed their last name to Carroll. They moved more than fifteen times. Mahulda, became the first Black female principal in Levy County, Although she had success in her career, she lived a terrified and miserable life because of her experiences that week in January 1923. "She never truly recovered from Rosewood," said her daughter Lizzie. In 1948, at the age of 53, Mahulda committed suicide. Aaron died 18 years later, in 1966, at the age of 70.

Emma Carrier, who was shot in the hand and the wrist during the riots, reached Gainesville by train. She never recovered and died in 1924.

Beulah (Scrappy) Carrier left Rosewood to become a singer in a traveling tent show, the "Florida Blossom Minstrels." She passed away in 1970 at age 70.

Sarah Carrier's husband Haywood did not see the events in Rosewood. He was on a hunting trip, and discovered when he returned that his wife, brother James, and son Sylvester had all been killed, and his house destroyed. Haywood rarely spoke to anyone but himself; he sometimes wandered away from his family unclothed. He died a year after the massacre at age 57.

Philomena Goins Doctor, the 11-year-old who accompanied her grandmother Sarah Carrier that New Year's morning to help wash clothes at Fannie Taylor's house and witnessed the White stranger enter Fannie Taylor's home, dropped out of school to care for her siblings. She became the featured singer for the Charles Bradley Band. She performed on stage with Ella Fitzgerald and Chick Webb and traveled to New York, Chicago, and other major cities. But there was a dark side to Philomena. Her weight ballooned to two-hundred-and-fifty pounds draped on a five-foot-two frame, and she was frequently bedridden with depression and had bouts of rage, once claiming God was standing at the foot of her bed. She became particularly depressed each Christmas, recounting the horrors she lived through. She died in 1991 at the age of 79.

Philomena's mother. Willie Retha Carrier Goins, died that same year. She was near 100 years old. It happened on Martin Luther King day. The family had gathered to celebrate. After a dinner of fried fish she excused herself to go to the bathroom for some Alka-Seltzer. She never came out. The paramedics were called, they tried reviving her, but she was gone.

Henry "Jack" Jackson Cason, the turpentine boss who helped thwart the mob lynching of Aaron Carrier, who was twice married and had thirteen children, died in 1951 at age 80.

Bryant Hudson, who shot and killed Sam Carter, died in a Veterans Hospital in Lake City, Florida in 1931 from injuries, friends say, he sustained in a fight. He was only 33 years old.

Arnold (he liked being called A.T.) Goins, Philomena's brother, was one of the children that got on the train for Gainesville. He stayed there for years before moving to St. Petersburg, where, during the depression, he dug ditches, laying down sewer pipe, then he made a living shining shoes for twenty cents a pair. He worked hard, saved his money, and put his daughter through college. She got her Ph.D., married a university president and moved to a house on a golf course, the same course Arnold caddied at 30 years earlier—back when no Blacks were allowed as members. A.T. died in 2002, at the age of 87.

After fleeing Rosewood, Lee Ruth Bradley Davis found her way to Miami, where she worked as a private nurse, a mailroom clerk at Lane Bryant (a clothing store for large-size women), and did odd jobs for the Dade County School Board. She retired in 1981. In 1992, at age seventy-seven, Lee Ruth recalled how "rough and hard" it had been those last days in Rosewood. "It is sometimes a nightmare to me," she said and credited the Lord for getting her through it all. A strong-willed woman of great religious faith, she went to church each day. Lee Ruth died in 1993 at the age of 78—months before the State of Florida would grant reparations to survivors of the massacre.

Ruben Mitchell, the boy who lost an eye in the siege at the Carrier home, moved to North Carolina and worked for Fieldcrest Mills in their sheeting division. He married Sadie May Freman. They had three children and six grandchildren. After a short illness he died in 1986, at the age of 76.

John Wright's house was the only structure left standing in Rosewood. His life was never the same after the attack. When word got out that he harbored some Blacks, he was vilified, called a "N***** lover," and his life threatened. He carried a pistol wherever he went and kept a pistol on every table in his house. When his wife died in 1931, John developed a problem with alcohol. He died after drinking too much one night in Cedar Key, and was buried in an unmarked grave in Sumner.

In 1925, after the sawmill in Sumner burned down ("Blazed up in a fire so huge the heat could be felt a quarter mile away"), the operation up and moved south. It wasn't unusual for the timber industry: come into an area, strip out all the good wood, then then a decade later, when the area is made barren of its precious resource, move on. Cummers did just that. They disassembled whatever was left standing, even taking the pipes that fed the back-porch sinks, loaded it all onto railroad flatcars and never looked back. Like a traveling gypsy circus, they simply moved on to the next hard-scrabble town, workers and all.

Some survivors as well as participants in the mob action went to Lacoochee to work in the mill there. Walter Pillsbury was among them, and he was taunted by former Sumner residents. No longer having any supervisory authority, Pillsbury was retired early by the company. He moved to Jacksonville and started his own operation, but was swindled out of business by associates. In 1926, while driving on a lonely country road, his car stalled. He got under the vehicle and fixed a leaking fuel line, but, not realizing it, some of the gasoline got on his clothes. He got back in the driver's seat, pulled out his pipe, lit a match, and was burned to death.

Ernest Parham, whose family ran the hotel in Sumner and had witnessed the horrors that week in Rosewood, married Walter Pillsbury's daughter and went on to run the biggest dry cleaning business in Orlando, Acme Cleaners and Laundry (it's still in operation, with the grandchildren now in charge). He provided a riveting account of the Rosewood Massacre to the Florida Legislature when it was considering reparations. Parham died at age 93 in 1997.

Jesse Hunter, the escaped convict and Fannie's accused attacker, was never found (if he ever existed at all).

★

Seventy years to the day after the Rosewood Massacre, on January 1, 1993, just outside Tampa, Florida, less than 100 miles from Rosewood, two White men, Mark Kohut and Charles Rourk, a pair of White trash day laborers who were roommates in a trailer park in the central Florida town of Lakeland, abducted 32-year-old Christopher Wilson, a Black tourist from Brooklyn who was visiting friends in Tampa.

They took him to a field, where he was robbed, taunted with racial slurs, doused with gasoline and set on fire. They left a note: "One less N*****, and more to go."

★

That same year, in 1993, seventy years after the Rosewood Riots, largely as a result of renewed interest based on then newly-published stories in the press, the Florida Legislature commissioned a report on the 1923 Rosewood incident.

The report called the massacre "a tragedy of American democracy and the American legal system" and noted that "the failure of elected white officials to take forceful actions to protect the safety and property of local black residents was part of a pattern in the state."

In 1994, the Florida Legislature put forward the Rosewood Bill. It was one of many that would be considered as part of the state's proposed $38 billion budget. There was a bill to castrate convicted rapists, one to pay women on welfare to use birth control, another to bar protestors from blockading abortion clinics, one to allow prayer in school and another to allow paddling, and there was even a bill to punish people who spread lies about Florida oranges.

The debate over the bill was heated (Lawmakers worried about being flooded with other reparation cases from different incidents, crowding the legislative agenda and draining the state's coffers). It the end, though, it was passed (71 to 40 in the house and 26 to 14 in the senate), but instead of the recommended $7 million in compensation, it became $1.5 million in reparations to survivors and another $500,000 pool to compensate for property losses. Later, a college scholarship fund was added (Since 1994, 297 students have received Rosewood scholarships).

Some 400 applications for compensation were received from around the world. The following year, the state distributed $150,000 checks to nine living survivors and through a complicated formula, dispersed the $500,000 in property money. Some descendants, after dividing the funds among their siblings, received not much more than $100 each.

One of the reparation recipients was the then 80-year-old Minnie Lee Langley. Minnie had moved to Jacksonville in 1926 and found work caring for babies. She married Clifford in 1936. He worked in a Firestone tire store, "changin' tires, changin' oil." When Minnie married Clifford, she had a six-year-old daughter, Dorothy, who Clifford raised like she was his own. He died of a heart attack in 1956. Minnie stopped working in 1980, after thirty two years on an assembly line at a brush and broom factory, where she started at 75 cents an hour, and worked her way up to $3.75 an hour by the time she retired (without a pension). When asked what she planned to do with the money, she said she might purchase a new sofa and a washer and dryer. "I ain't never been crazy about money," she explained. "I worked all my life, I worked hard, and I made what I needed. I made money, but money ain't never made me. It would never change me. Not money, not nothin' gonna' get between me and the Lord. Minnie passed away less than two years later.

Robie Mortin also received $150,000. She bought herself a brand new 1995 Cutlass Supreme. After Rosewood, Robie got married, twice, had five children, moved to Riviera Beach in southern Florida, and spent the next few decades cleaning the houses of the rich and famous on Palm Beach Island. "Worked for them Pulitzers (Herbert Pulitzer was the wealthy grandson of publishing magnate Joseph Pulitzer. He famously married Roxanne Dixon, 21 years younger, a former cheerleader. Their divorce set tongues wagging when both Pulitzers claimed that they had shared in sexual encounters with Jacquie Kimberly, socialite wife of Kleenex heir James Kimberly) for eighteen years … started out as a laundress, and wound up doing everything—cookin' cleanin', and the parties, a lot of parties!" She passed away in 2010 after a brief illness. She was 94.

Another Rosewood survivor to receive $150,000 was Wilson Hall. He was only seven in 1923. He and his family ended up in Gainesville, in a two-room tar-paper shack behind an icehouse near the railroad station. Big for his age, at 13 years old he got a job sparring at a local gym for five dollars a session, until his mother made him quit. For the next several decades of his adult life he moved around. For almost 40 years he worked as a janitor in a movie studio storage facility in Chicago. By the mid-1980s he landed in a tiny northern Florida town running a tiny nightclub—crammed between a taxidermist and the Dixie Motel, which consisted of little more than a pool table and three tattered booths, but it was his. The jukebox was filled with the best blues and jazz records around. He died in 1998 at the age of 82 due to complications from a stroke. The reparation money wasn't that important to him, said his wife Stephanie. He wanted the truth known about Rosewood, she said. "He was robbed of his heritage."

Willie Evans also got a $150,000 check. His grandfather, Ransom Edwards and his wife, Julia, owned a small farm on the fringe of Rosewood. The elderly Ransom, who was the segregated school's superintendent, was called "cantankerous and irritably aloof." Julia was a housekeeper for some of the women in Sumner. When the riots began, they fled to the woods with Willie. Willie eventually settled in San-ford, Florida. Like other survivors, he said very little about the night in 1923. Willie had retired in 1968 after he went blind. He had spent twenty years sawing cement and bricks, dust and chips flying into his face eight hours a day—for sixteen dollars a day. After his money arrived, he put in new windows ("The termites been eatin' it up pretty bad"), fixed up his front porch and bought a "Lazy-boy" chair ("You know, that lift you up, stretch your feet out, lay you back.") so he could listen to his favorite TV show, "The Price is Right." Willie died at age 99 in 2007.

Lonnie Jefferson (Carrier) Carroll, James and Emma Carrier's son, was twelve when the Rosewood Massacre happened. He was at the Carrier house that Thurs-day night. Lonnie, who raked pine straw in his youth, became a logger, "following the wood," said his wife Lugenia. Mostly he worked in the forests around Palatka, halfway between Gainesville and the Atlantic. He was a big man, six-foot-two and two hundred pounds—strong enough to have earned extra money boxing, for "four dollars a fight," said Lugenia. "That's what they paid him. When he had a stroke, Lonnie ended up in the Ocean View Nursing Home, where he spent most days lying in bed, blind, his face partially paralyzed. The money he received paid for a new Frigidaire and air conditioning for the house Lugenia lived in. "Nothing much changed," she said. "We're just goin' on living." Lonnie died at age 83 in 1997.

When word got out that survivors received a $150,000 cash settlement, Doro-thy Hosey was overrun with relatives—some she didn't know she had—calling her, knocking on her door, asking for money, demanding their share, cursing her if she resisted. She bought a house, got an unlisted phone number and went into hiding. Dorothy died in 2005 at the age of 86.

Wilson's Hall's mother, Mary, with little education, had to resort to a lot of begging that first year they were on their own in Gainesville. Eventually she found work as a maid and cook, often bringing leftover food home to feed her children. Mary took another husband, Henry Price, but she never recovered all that she lost in Rosewood. Like many survivors, she was held prisoner by her memories of that week of terror. It was a subject too painful to discuss. When she was awarded the $150,000, she moved from her tiny apartment into a home she bought with the proceeds. She got an unlisted phone number, too, after being harassed. "It's the young people," she said, "I've never been close to any of them. They're lookin' at me now like I cheated them out of something, like I got something they should've had." Mary died at the age of 98 in Jacksonville in 2018. As her granddaughter Alzada Hall-Harrell recalled, "She always told me, 'don't ever lie. I can't stand a lie, because one person tellin' a lie started that whole disaster.'"

In June 2020, Vera Goins-Hamilton, granddaughter of Sarah Carrier and Philomena's and A.T.'s sister, who was two years old when the Rosewood Massacre happened, died at the age of 100. The night of the shooting at the Carrier house she was with her parents at a logging camp in Otter Creek. When Vera had a child at fourteen, she moved to Lacoochee, where she stayed for the next fifty years—through three husbands, two children, five grandchildren and one great-grandchild. During the war, Vera got a job on the assembly line at the Pasco Packing plant down in Dade City, the largest citrus packing plant in the world. After the war she ran a jook joint out of her home, serving the best homecooked food around. In the early 1950s, she left the bar business and cleaned the houses of White families, then, eventually became a housekeeper at a Holiday Inn off the new interstate highway, until she retired in 1993. So worried about reprisal her whole life, she never claimed her right to any of the state compensation fund and never publicly talked about her Rosewood history. She took whatever memories she had to the grave.

Philomena's son, Arnett Doctor, heard about Rosewood for the first time when he was a young boy growing up in Lacoochee. One Christmas his mother told him about the week of violence that destroyed the town. She made him promise never to speak of it. However, after serving 12 years in the Army and later owning a cleaning company, he retired and devoted himself to seeking reparations for the Rosewood survivors—much to his mother's consternation. After a long illness, Arnett died in 2015 at the age of 72.

In a 1993 interview, Arnett insisted that Sylvester Carrier did not die that night in Rosewood, that he was smuggled out of town in a coffin (concealed under a dead body) and later lived in Texas and Louisiana, and, as proof, he offered up that his mother received Christmas cards from her brother up until 1964. When asked about the existence of the cards, Arnett claimed his mother threw them away years earlier.

Like many stories told by survivors and their descendants about the events that took place that awful week in Rosewood, with the passage of time, with memories faded and tales told and retold, this one could never be proven. It hardly mattered, though. Whether Sylvester died that night in January 1923 or sometime later, he fought heroically against the odious curse of racial violence—and that's all you can ask of any one human being.

In 2004, the State of Florida declared Rosewood a Florida Heritage Landmark in and subsequently erected a modest historical marker on State Road 24 that names the victims and describes the community's destruction. If you blink, you'll miss it.

★

Back in 1993, when the State of Florida was considering paying reparations to survivors, a reporter went to what was once Rosewood. Next to the only seemingly-occupied structure around, a rust-stained ramshackle trailer, was Wesley Thomson. Leaning against a battered pickup truck, its wheels planted in weeds, beer in hand, he remarked, "That what happened was in 1932 or 1923, or whenever it was … N***** done shot a white man. That's what started it all. Naturally they all come down and started killin' after that."

With talk about Rosewood descendants wanting compensation, he exclaims, "I bought this place in 'seventy-two'—from the timber company, that's where my deed come from. These N*****s talking all about how this land was theirs and they're owed something for it? Are you kiddin' me? These people didn't own no land. Shit, *they* was owned!

Wesley's wife, Christy Thompson, a big brassy brunette clad in shorts, T-shirt and flip-flops, declared, "I don't think it was right what they done. These coloreds were human just like we are. But I don't think these ones out there now [the survivors] ought to be reapin' all the profit off it either, not when there's other families that suffered from this, too, *white* families, and nobody's said *diddley squat* about them, and they're not speakin' for themselves because they just want to let the past *die*."

★

Noted journalist and author, Pierre Berton, once wrote "Racism is a refuge for the ignorant. It seeks to divide and to destroy. It is the enemy of freedom, and deserves to be met head-on and stamped out."

Racism didn't stop with the Rosewood Massacre. Racism had wrapped itself so tightly around the primal fears of our society that it choked all reason and feeling from the atmosphere.

The Scottsboro case was a prime example of how stubbornly deep-rooted racism had become in America in the twentieth century that it was able to pervert the justice system. The Scottsboro Boys were nine Black Alabama teenagers falsely charged with raping two White women on a train in 1931.

The two alleged victims were hardly the virtuous women the state had tried to portray them to be. They were prostitutes who had concocted the charges out of thin air. One eventually recanted her testimony.

The defendants were not given lawyers until the morning of the trial and their attorneys made almost no effort to defend their clients. The young men were fortunate to barely escaped a lynch mob sent to kill them, but were railroaded into convictions and death sentences. The Supreme Court overturned the convictions on the basis of effective representation.

Still, Alabama insisted on retrying the defendants. This time, Samuel Leibowitz, one of the premier defense attorneys of the day, came to represent the Scottsboro nine. It didn't matter. The jury, all White men because Black men were systematically excluded, convicted them once again.

In fact, there would be many more trials of the Scottsboro defendants over the years and each time the jury convicted and was later reversed on appeal. When the saga finally ended, all of the defendants were released. But not until they had served an average of a decade for the phantom crime.

★

Beginning in 1933, when Adolf Hitler and the Nazi party came to power in Germany, Black activists and the Black press used White America's condemnation of Nazi bigotry to expose the abuses of Jim Crow racism at home.

In 1935, Nazi Germany passed two radically discriminatory pieces of legislation, collectively known as the Nuremberg Laws, which laid the legal groundwork for the persecution of Jewish people during the Holocaust and World War II, to legally disenfranchise and discriminate against a class of citizens.

Ironically, the Nazis looked to American race law, like "one drop" rules, which stipulated that anyone with any Black ancestry was legally Black and could not marry a White person (notably, Virginia had a "Pocahontas Exception" for prominent White families who claimed to be descended from the favorite daughter of Powhatan, the formidable ruler of the Algonquian tribes).

The comparisons were striking. In the segregated American South, racist laws banning Blacks from public places such as libraries and swimming pools were instituted at the local level. In Germany, laws placing similar prohibitions on Jews were also, at least initially, a matter of municipal control.

"In the freest country in the world," noted a Nazi newspaper, "where even the president rages against racial discrimination, no citizen of dark color is permitted to travel next to a white person, even if the white is employed as a sewer digger and the Negro is a world boxing champion or otherwise a national hero...[this] example shows us all how we have to solve the problem of traveling foreign Jews."

★

When America officially entered World War II in late 1941, once more believing—hoping against hope—that fighting for American democracy abroad would grant Blacks full citizenship at home, Blacks volunteered in record numbers. One million Black soldiers would fight with valor against the Axis powers in every theater of the war.

Doris Miller, a Navy mess attendant (he served breakfast and collected laundry), was the first Black recipient of the Navy Cross, awarded for his actions during the attack on Pearl Harbor. Miller had voluntarily manned an anti-aircraft gun and fired at the Japanese aircraft, despite having no prior training in the weapon's use.

On D-Day, the First Army on Omaha and Utah Beaches included about 1,700 Black troops. The all-Black 761st Tank Battalion fought its way through France with Patton's Third Army, spending 183 days in combat. They were credited with capturing 30 major towns in France, Belgium, and Germany.

A 1925 War Department study concluded that Blacks were temperamentally and biologically unsuited to become pilots. Under pressure from civil rights groups and with the powerful intervention of Eleanor Roosevelt, an "experiment" began at Tuskegee Institute in Alabama to train Black pilots for the U. S. Army Air Forces. Many critics, including army brass, hoped the experiment would fail.

Four hundred and fifty Black fighter pilots, under the command of Col Benjamin O. Davis, Jr., who would go on to become the U.S. Air Force's first Black general, fought in the aerial war over North Africa, Sicily, and Europe.

The all-Black Tuskegee Airmen flew 1,578 combat missions and 179 bomber escort missions, destroying 112 enemy aircraft in the air, another 150 on the ground and damaged another 148, wrecked 40 boats and barges, plus demolished 950 rail cars, trucks and other motor vehicles and put one destroyer out of action.

Sixty-six of these pilots were killed in aircraft accidents or in aerial combat while another thirty-two were shot down and captured as prisoners of war. The returning airman earned 150 Distinguished Flying Crosses, a Legion of Merit, 744 Air Medals, 8 Purple Hearts, 2 Soldiers Medals, 14 Bronze stars and a Red Star of Yugoslavia.

The Tuskegee airman, though, were a rare exception. Most Black soldiers ended up serving in labor and supply units, rather than combat units—as the military, dominated by White Southern officers, argued that mixing of the races would undermine military efficiency and negatively impact the morale of White soldiers.

Except for a few short weeks during the Battle of the Bulge in the winter of 1944 when commanders were desperate for manpower, all U.S. soldiers served in strictly segregated units. Even the blood banks were segregated.

★

While Blacks were fighting and dying thousands of miles away, fights were breaking out back home—in places like Detroit.

The apparent industrial prosperity that made Detroit the "Arsenal of Democracy," almost three million people crowded in and around the nation's then fourth-largest city, masked a deeper social unrest that erupted during the summer of 1943.

Because Black Detroiters were treated as second class citizens, they suffered disproportionately from wartime rationing and the overall strains on the city. Black workers faced virulent racism. At many factories, Whites refused to work alongside Blacks. Housing was limited—by design. Detroit's 200,000 Black residents were confined to sixty square blocks in two areas known as "Paradise Valley" and "Black Bottom." Many lived in homes without indoor plumbing, yet they paid rent two to three times higher than families in White neighborhoods.

On June 20, 1943, with temperatures at 90 degrees and tempers heated up as well, hostilities finally boiled over, as some two hundred Blacks and Whites fought in the street. Though police quelled the violence, tensions continued.

Rumors quickly swirled at the Forest Social Club in Paradise Valley that Whites had thrown a Black woman and her baby off of the Belle Isle Bridge. A furious mob of 500 was formed that moved through downtown Detroit, breaking windows, looting White businesses, and attacking White individuals.

In a nearby area, angry Whites had gathered after allegations were made of Blacks raping a White woman near the same bridge. A mob of White men formed outside the Roxy Theatre in the downtown area, and when the movie let out, Black men were set upon and beaten. White police reportedly told Black bystanders to "run and not look back." Some were shot from behind.

Gangs of each color roamed the streets, White mobs overturned cars owned by Blacks and set them on fire, a White doctor was beaten to death while making a house call in a Black neighborhood and Whites beat Black men as White policemen looked on. After one police beating, one Black victim asked to be taken to a hospital. "N*****s don't need doctors," the cop told him.

Violence was curbed by the arrival of 6,000 army troops in tanks armed with automatic weapons. The toll was appalling, though. The 36 hours of rioting claimed 34 lives, 25 of them Black. More than 1,800 were arrested for looting and other incidents, the vast majority Black. Thirteen of the murders remained unsolved.

★

By 1947, with a Cold War brewing, the reality of the segregated Jim Crow occupational army in Germany was becoming a major embarrassment for the U.S. government. The Soviet Union and East German communist propaganda relentlessly attacked America and challenged its claim to be the leader of the "free world."

Under the red hot spotlight, in July 1948, President Harry Truman signed Executive Order 9981, desegregating the armed forces. Truman declared, "there shall be equality of treatment and opportunity for all persons in the armed services without regard to race, color, religion or national origin."

Those were nice words on paper, but, in reality, very little effectively changed for Black GIs. Much of the armed forces during the Korean conflict, for instance, remained segregated.

North Korean propaganda pamphlets touted, "Between January 1950 and June 1951, 85 Negros have been lynched in the United States ... NEGRO SOLDIERS! You've got a fight on your hands at home. Don't come fighting coloured people out here!"

Six hundred thousand Black soldiers over the course of the Korean conflict served, from a segregated society, in a segregated army—forgotten soldiers in America's "forgotten war."

One Black unit, in particular, was singled out as the reason segregation was necessary. The all-Black 24th Infantry Regiment was one of several outnumbered American units overwhelmed by a surprise attack, when 300,000 Chinese troops stormed across the Yalu River on November 24, 1950. Many Americans were killed, wounded or captured in the attack. It almost cost the U.S. the war.

As a result, the U.S. Army chose to disband this one Black unit, singling it out for cowardice, accusing the Black soldiers of being "untrustworthy and incapable of carrying out missions expected of an infantry regiment." When American dead were buried in a military cemetery near Seoul, the 24th's unit marker was painted yellow.

There were numerous White units who performed just as poorly, too, but their botched efforts were excused away.

The debate would rage on for decades. At one point a group of Black veterans threatened a defamation suit against the Pentagon in an effort to block publication of an official history describing failures by the Army's last Black combat regiment.

The book was published anyway in 1996. The 314-page document reads like it was written a century earlier: "There was no single reason for what happened … failures in the 24th tended to be attributed less to their military causes than to the race of the unit's soldiers. Blacks were afraid of the dark … they would not dig foxholes, and they lacked the innate intelligence to keep their equipment in good repair."

★

In 1955, 14-year-old Emmitt Till, a Black student on summer break visiting his family in Mississippi from Chicago, decided to walk down to a store to buy candy. On the way out he was supposedly heard saying, "Bye, baby" to 21-year-old Carolyn Bryant. That was all it took for him to lose his life.

Bryant's husband Roy, and his half-brother, J. W. Milam, kidnapped Till from his uncle's house, beat him, tortured him, shot him in the head, tied his body up with barbed wire, hung him and threw the remains into the Tallahatchie River. Bryant and Milam, were quickly arrested and charged with murder.

Till's corpse was so disfigured that his uncle could only identify it by an initialed ring. Till's mother requested the body be sent back to Chicago. After seeing the mutilated remains, she decided to have an open-casket funeral to show the world what racist murderers had done to her son. *Jet* magazine published a photo of the corpse. Soon the mainstream media picked up on the story.

The trial was a mockery. In spite of the fact that eyewitnesses positively identified the pair, an all-White jury deliberated for less than an hour before issuing a verdict of "not guilty." With the double-jeopardy laws protecting them, Bryant and Milam agreed to be interviewed by *Look* magazine (for a $4,000 fee), proudly admitting to the killing. Milam said he did it "just so everybody can know how me and my folks stand."

Over the years, Emmitt Till's gravesite was such a frequent target for racist vandalism and theft, that in 2019 authorities replaced it with a bulletproof tombstone.

★

Through the second half of the 1950s and into the 1960s, the nation would witness many historic events that would help shape civil rights for decades to come. In 1955, after Rosa Parks was arrested for refusing to give up her seat on a Montgomery, Alabama bus to a White man, Blacks led a year-long citywide boycott.

In early 1960, four Black college students took a stand against segregation in Greensboro, North Carolina when they refused to leave a Woolworth's lunch counter without being served. Other sit-ins would follow.

In 1961, an assembly of Black and White civil rights activists held "freedom rides" on buses across the South to test a US Supreme Court ruling forbidding segregated facilities in interstate transport. In May 1963, TV viewers watched in horror as police used fire hoses and attack dogs against peaceful protesters in Birmingham, Alabama, many of whom were children. It prompted President Kennedy (who would be assassinated later that year) to propose a comprehensive civil rights bill.

That same month, activist Medgar Evers, who challenged the segregation of the state-supported public University of Mississippi, would be gunned down in his driveway by Byron De La Beckwith Jr., a White supremacist and Klansman (after two trials, both with hung juries, 31 years later, based on new evidence, Beckwith was tried once more, convicted of the murder and sentenced to life in prison).

In 1965, Malcolm X, a Black nationalist—considered by some a heroic advocate for the rights of Blacks, where others saw him as a racist who openly promoted violence (who famously said, "We didn't land on Plymouth Rock, Plymouth Rock landed on us.")—would die in a hail of bullets by rival Black Muslims while giving a speech in a Harlem ballroom.

The next few years had a prickly air about them, when a simmering cauldron of racial tension exploded into what was called the 1967 Detroit Riot. Racial profiling and police brutality were commonplace back then.

In the wee hours of July 23, police raided a party above the Economy Printing Shop at the corner of 12th and Clairmount. The party was for two soldiers returning from the Vietnam War. The location was known by police as a site of a "blind pig," slang for an unlicensed bar.

An angry crowd would retaliate against police, setting off mayhem that included heavy looting, sniping, and arson. It resulted in 43 dead, several thousand injuries and more than 4,000 arrests during an emergency period. Fire heavily damaged residential and commercial areas, including blocks of small businesses.

In 1967, the Kerner Commission investigated the causes of race rioting that year (such as the Detroit riots). In its findings published in 1968, it found that poverty and institutional racism were driving inner-city violence, that America was moving towards two societies—one Black, one White; separate and unequal; it blamed the rioting on a lack of access to adequate housing, education, and employment opportunities, and cited aggressive police tactics and the abrasive relationship between the police and the minority communities as an explosive source of grievance, tension and disorder.

The commission called for steep increases in federal aid to the cities, a federal jobs program to employ one million workers, and an increase in the minimum wage, among other redistributive policy proposals. President Johnson wholly rejected the Commission's recommendations.

★

In the early evening of April 4, 1968, the Reverend Martin Luther King, Nobel Peace Prize recipient for his nonviolent stand on racial inequality and the very public face of the civil rights movement, was standing on the balcony at the Lorraine Motel in Memphis, Tennessee. King had been in town to support 1,300 Black sanitation workers who had gone on strike over unequal wages and working conditions. He was about to head out to dinner with friends.

James Earl Ray, a White small-time criminal who escaped from a Missouri prison a year earlier, drove his white Ford Mustang to Memphis from Atlanta, and rented a room in a boarding house directly across the street from the motel, checking in under the alias John Willard, He lay in wait. When King emerged from room 306 at 6:01pm, Ray steadied his rifle, took aim and fired. The 30-06 bullet entered King's right jaw, traveled through his neck, severing his spinal cord. Doctors at St. Joseph Hospital attempted emergency surgery but the wound was too serious. He died at 7:05pm. He was only 39 years old.

The night before, King had prophesized his death in a speech delivered at a rally: "…I got to Memphis. And some began to say the threats, or talk about the threats that were out…We've got some difficult days ahead. But it doesn't matter with me now. Because I've been to the mountaintop. And I don't mind. Like anybody, I would like to live a long life. Longevity has its place. But I'm not concerned about that now. I just want to do God's will. And He's allowed me to go up to the mountain. And I've looked over. And I've seen the promised land. I may not get there with you. But I want you to know tonight, that we, as a people, will get to the promised land. So I'm happy, tonight. I'm not worried about anything. I'm not fearing any man. Mine eyes have seen the glory of the coming of the Lord."

With King's death, many Blacks felt hope for a better life had died with him. It was an uneasy summer as civil disturbances broke out in some 100 cities across the country.

★

In Martin Luther's King's 1963 speech at the Lincoln Memorial, he said he had a dream that one day the sons of former slaves and sons of slave owners would sit at the same table. Of all places, that dream would come true on the front lines of the Vietnam War.

Just because they fought side by side, though, didn't mean the races got along. On the contrary, when news of King's death reached Vietnam, there were reports of White GIs hanging Confederate battle flags outside their barracks in celebration. The Army and the Marines briefly banned the flag raisings, but it was overturned when Southern politicians objected. There were at least three confirmed cross burnings.

Eventually, military leaders were forced to investigate. Not too surprisingly, they largely focused on the responsibility of Black soldiers for these incidents. In late 1969, Deputy Assistant Secretary Bennett drew up recommendations that acknowledged that ignoring complaints of racial discrimination contributed to racial tension and violence. But military leaders ignored his proposals, and when Bennett's successor, Frank Render III, reached similar conclusions, he was promptly fired.

In the coming decades, embittered memories of the war—of inherent bias in the draft, discriminatory treatment in the armed forces, and institutional racism in all branches of the services, as well as poor treatment of Black veterans—soured many Blacks on military service. For Blacks, the legacy of Vietnam was "no more Vietnams."

★

With the Vietnam War over, with several federal acts of legislation established to protect the rights of all Americans, the late 1970s marked a period when many people were buoyant that racial tensions in American culture were on the mend. Any such notions, however, were quickly disabused.

In December 1979, a number of White Miami-Dade Florida police officers were involved in a high-speed chase of a Black motorist, Arthur McDuffie. Police reports said that the chase ended when McDuffie crashed his motorcycle, ultimately leading to his death.

A coroner report suggested otherwise. Later, a responding officer following the chase testified that there was no crash. The police officers had beaten McDuffie to death with their flashlights.

In spite of what the coroner said and the testimony from police and witnesses, an all-White jury acquitted all the officers involved. News spread to the surrounding areas and residents of Liberty City, home to half of the city's Black and Afro-West Indian residents, then took to the streets in protests which soon turned violent.

By nightfall, the violence escalated into a full blown riot as angry Blacks attacked motorists fleeing their vehicles. The riot moved into neighboring White business districts. The Florida National Guard was called in and order was restored. Ten Blacks and eight Whites died in the Riot.

★

In 1992, Rodney King, a 33-year-old Black man, was arrested for drunk driving following a high-speed chase. LAPD cops kicked the unarmed King repeatedly and beat him with batons for a reported 15 minutes as more than a dozen cops stood by and watched. The entire episode was caught on camera by a bystander and broadcast to the world. Unrest erupted in the city. More than 50 people died.

After all those involved were found innocent, Congress gave the Justice Department the authority to investigate a pattern or practice of policing that violated civil rights protections. More than two decades after Congress created the Department of Justice's authority to investigate and remedy systemic police misconduct. The Division had just 18 open reform agreements, five open investigations, and one case in active litigation.

★

On June 21, 2005, Edgar Ray Killen, a Ku Klux Klan organizer who planned and directed the murders of James Chaney, Andrew Goodman, and Michael Schwerner, three civil rights activists participating in the Freedom Summer of 1964, was convicted of manslaughter on the 41st anniversary of the crimes.

In February 2007, Emmett Till's 1955 murder case, which was reopened by the Department of Justice in 2004, was officially closed. The two confessed murderers, J. W. Milam and Roy Bryant, were dead of cancer by 1994, and prosecutors lacked sufficient evidence to pursue further convictions.

★

The term "Black Lives Matter" was first used by organizer Alicia Garza in a July 2013 Facebook post in response to the acquittal of George Zimmerman, a Florida man who shot and killed unarmed 17-year-old Trayvon Martin on February 26, 2012.

More than a hashtag, Black Lives Matter has become an anthem to raise awareness that every person's life is important; to speak out against the police brutality and systemic racism; to eradicate White supremacy and intervene in violence inflicted on Black communities through advocacy and education. Their voices have been called upon many times in recent years.

On July 17, 2014, Eric Garner was murdered in the New York City borough of Staten Island after Daniel Pantaleo, a New York City Police Department officer, put him in a chokehold while arresting him (despite chokeholds being banned in NYPD since 1993).

Video footage of the incident (Garner belly down on the sidewalk, repeating "I can't breathe" until he lost consciousness and died) generated widespread national attention and raised questions about the appropriate use of force by law enforcement.

A month later, on August 9, 2014, Michael Brown Jr., an 18-year-old Black man, was fatally shot and killed by 28-year-old White police officer, Darren Wilson, in the city of Ferguson, Missouri, a suburb of St. Louis. The shooting prompted protests that roiled the area for weeks. "Hands up, don't shoot" becoming a national slogan.

Three months later the St. Louis County prosecutor announced that a grand jury decided not to indict Wilson. It set off another wave of protests. In March, the Justice Department called on Ferguson to overhaul its criminal justice system, declaring that the city had engaged in constitutional violations.

★

In spite of the outrage and demonstrations, the same kind of story kept repeating itself: the callous, cold-blooded killing of Black men, women and trans women.

On March 13, 2020, shortly after midnight, Breonna Taylor, a 26-year-old Black emergency medical technician, was fatally shot by Louisville Kentucky plainclothes police officers who were executing a no-knock search warrant, supposedly looking for a stash of drugs. Gunfire was exchanged between Taylor's boyfriend and the officers. Taylor was hit eight times. No drugs were found in the apartment.

Walker told investigators that Breonna struggled to breathe for at least five minutes after she was shot, and received no medical attention for more than 20 minutes.

The boyfriend, who was licensed to carry a weapon, was arrested and charged with the attempted murder of a police officer (the charges were later dropped). Officer Bretty Hankison, who showed "extreme indifference to the value of human life" when he "blindly fired 10 rounds into the back of Taylor's apartment and the one next door without verifying they were directed against someone who posed an immediate threat," was eventually terminated from the police force, but the other two cops involved were only suspended pending an investigation that, as of the publication of this book, is still on-going. None have been charged with a crime.

"The most disrespected person in America is the black woman," said Malcolm X in 1962. "The most unprotected person in America is the black woman. The most neglected person in America is the black woman."

The first half of 2020 witnessed at least 25 transgender or gender non-conforming people fatally shot or killed by other violent means, which is almost as many such killings as all of 2019.

Two Black transgender women were killed in June 2020—during gay pride month—within days of each other. In Liberty Township, Ohio, 25-year-old Riah Milton was lured to a park by a 14-year-old girl and two men in an apparent attempt to steal her car, during which she was shot several times and was left to die.

A day earlier, 27-year-old Dominique "Rem'Mie" Fells was found dead from multiple stab wounds, the remains found alongside the Schuylkill River in the Bartam's Garden area of Philadelphia. Both of the victim's legs were cut off at the upper thighs.

★

On May 25, 2020, 46-year-old George Floyd died after being handcuffed and pinned to the ground by White Minneapolis police officer Derek Chauvin. Chauvin was filmed kneeling on Floyd's neck for almost eight full minutes.

Floyd had been accused of using a counterfeit $20 bill at Cup Foods, a local grocery store. His death would become a cause célèbre for the Black Lives Matter movement.

Transcripts of police bodycam footage show Floyd said more than 20 times he could not breathe as he was restrained by the officers. "Please, I can't breathe," Floyd kept saying.

"Can't believe this, man," he uttered. "Mom, love you. Love you. Tell my kids I love them. I'm dead."

One woman told the police: "His nose is bleeding, come on now!" When bystanders confronted the officers about Floyd's condition, Chauvin pulled out a can of mace to keep them at bay.

Soon Floyd became silent and non-responsive. A few in the crowd urged the officers to check his pulse.

One officer did, but "couldn't find one." Yet the police did nothing.

Finally, eight minutes into being pinned to the pavement, Chauvin removed his knee from Floyd's neck. By then it was too late. Floyd was dead.

Police initially claimed that Floyd "suffered a medical episode while struggling with officers," but the bystander's video proved that was a lie.

After enormous public pressure was applied, all four officers involved in the Floyd incident were fired. Chauvin was charged with second-degree murder and the three others were charged with aiding and abetting second-degree murder.

As a *New York Times* roundtable discussion on the killing pointed out, "[George Floyd's] death has touched off the largest and most sustained round of protests the country has seen since the 1960s, as well as demonstrations around the world. The killing has also prompted renewed calls to address brutality, racial disparities and impunity in American policing—and beyond that, to change the conditions that burden black and Latino communities."

Just two weeks after the George Floyd killing, the police chief in Minneapolis withdrew the department from contract negotiations with the union. The big bone of contention wasn't salaries; it was the use of force and the discipline process.

★

When Nancy Green died on August 30, 1923—the same year as the Rosewood Massacre—as a result of a car that collided with a laundry truck and "hurtled" itself onto a Chicago sidewalk where she was standing, she had been the face of the Aunt Jemima brand of pancake mix and syrup for over three decades.

Nancy Green's living trademark "mammy" look would continue for almost a century more (although softened over the years), until in June 2020, when Quaker Oats, the brand's owner, announced it would retire the name and logo as it worked "to make progress toward racial equality" (The makers of Uncle Ben's rice and Mrs. Buttersworth made similar announcements).

The recent name change decision by Quaker Oats didn't come out of corporate largesse or some come-to-Jesus moment over racial sensitivity. Rather, it was as a result of sustained, widespread protests against racism that have reverberated throughout the country, pressuring changes in the corporate world.

And it's not as though the company wasn't aware that the image of a slave woman on a plantation (ironically, Green had been born a slave and worked on a plantation before being freed following the Civil War) offended many people. They knew, they had owned the brand for some 90 years, they'd heard the criticism and, in fact, had talked about "rebranding" in 2016, but nothing came of it.

Some people might say, what's the big deal, after all, it's only pancake mix and syrup. No, it's not. It's racism, pure and simple. Would we allow a company to sell "Hitler oven cleaner"? Of course not. So why would we allow a company to sell some food product that demeans Black people by implying that it was created by slaves to serve their White masters (which was the back story the founders created and perpetuated)? We shouldn't.

Racism, any racism, no matter how seemingly "innocent" or inadvertent, is racism. The deep racial and ethnic inequities that exist today are a direct result of structural racism: the historical and contemporary policies, practices, and norms that create and maintain White supremacy. Anything that furthers that agenda is wrong. Anything.

To break that cycle we need to see racism for what it is, acknowledge its existence, promote a public dialogue, and use our collective voices to help drown out the noise from those who chose to preach hate. If we don't, who will?

There's a well-known poetic "confession" made by a German Lutheran pastor, Martin Niemöller, who was a Nazi supporter when Hitler first came to power, but quickly grew disillusioned. He became the leader of a group of German clergymen opposed to Hitler. He wrote: "First they came for the socialists, and I did not speak out—Because I was not a socialist. Then they came for the trade unionists, and I did not speak out—Because I was not a trade unionist. Then they came for the Jews, and I did not speak out. Because I was not a Jew. Then they came for me—and there was no one left to speak for me."

This is what compelled me to write this book, for as Martin Luther King once said, "The ultimate measure of a person is not where one stands in moments of comfort and convenience, but where one stands in the times of challenge and controversy."

Anti-lynching crusader, Ida B. Wells, once wrote, "The way to right wrongs is to turn the light of truth upon them."

★

For millions of migrants, like my grandparents who escaped the pogroms in Russia at the turn of the twentieth century, America was the land of milk and honey. It offered freedom and unbounded opportunity.

After a week or two at sea with little to do but stare out at a vast ocean, jammed into steerage—or if they were lucky, in a third-class cabin, they stood on the deck as the ship steamed into the harbor, excited to capture that first glimpse of the promised land. Whistles blowing, people cheering, waving tiny flags, then it came into sight: the majestic Statue of Liberty, a figure of Libertas, a robed Roman liberty goddess. Those words by the poet Emma Lazarus (herself an immigrant) cried out:

"Give me your tired, your poor,
Your huddled masses yearning to breathe free,
The wretched refuse of your teeming shore.
Send these, the homeless, tempest-tost to me,
I lift my lamp beside the golden door!"

★

There is no record of what the first slaves brought to America were thinking. One can only imagine. Locked away in a dark, dank cargo hold for months, shackled together, packed in cheek by jowl with no room to turn, stacked sometimes seven high with less than three feet of headroom—the heat, the stench, the sickness and death, then hauled on deck filthy and nearly naked, to see a strange land of White people in their fancy clothes, staring at them as though they were wild savages. For them, there was no freedom, no opportunity, only a life of hardship and inescapable death. For them, freedom came at a high price. As Harriet Tubman wrote:

If you hear the dog. KEEP GOING. If you see the torches in the woods. KEEP GOING. If there's shouting after you. KEEP GOING. Don't ever stop. KEEP GOING. If you want to taste freedom. KEEP GOING.

★

It was June 17, 2015. A small group of Black churchgoers at the Emanuel African Methodist Episcopal Church in Charlotte, North Carolina was about to start evening Bible study when a quiet young White man walked in and was offered a seat. He sat in silence among the parishioners—his head hung low—for about 40 minutes, while the group considered the Gospel of Mark's account of the Parable of the Sower.

Then, as the gathered rose, their eyes clenched shut for a benediction, 21-year-old Dylann Roof pulled out a 45-caliber Glock handgun and began a bloody, senseless shooting spree, firing some 70 rounds. He killed nine Black churchgoers and wounded one. Each victim was hit repeatedly, with the eldest, Susie Jackson, an 87-year-old grandmother and church matriarch, struck at least 10 times.

Roof was quickly caught and would face justice. Fifty-nine-year-old hairstylist, Felicia Sanders, one of three survivors, told a packed courtroom that because of Dylann Roof, she can no longer close her eyes to pray. She had been forced to play dead by lying in her 26-year-old dying son's blood while holding her hand over her whimpering 11-year-old granddaughter's mouth. She had pressed her hand down so tight that she said she feared she would suffocate the child.

Dylann Roof, the expressionless loner, the moppy blond-haired, bug-eyed ninth-grade dropout, the unrepentant and inscrutable White supremacist who went on a brazen racial rampage, was unmoved. He was convicted and condemned to death by a federal jury.

After his verdict and sentencing, Roof wrote in his journal: "You blacks are killing white people on the streets every day and raping white women every day … I would like to make it crystal clear. I do not regret what I did. I am not sorry. I have not shed a tear for the innocent people I killed."

Why would a young man born of so much privilege, who never had to want for anything, who never felt the sting of racism against his cheek, target Black people he never met, and in all places, a house of worship? Because he felt he could. That's the easy answer. Moreover, he actually believed his sentence didn't matter because White nationalists would free him from prison after an impending race war he would help start.

How, then, do we break the cycle of racial hate that creates a Dylann Roof, how do we stop the needless violence, how do we prevent more senseless killings? How?

I wish I knew—but I don't. What I do know is that there is a sharp racial dividing line in America. It's not one you can see, though, or even put your finger on, but it's there, nonetheless.

On one side, are all those ready to repudiate this nation's long and ugly history of structural racism, to denounce evil, to join together with outstretched hands in devotion with all humankind.

On the other side, are those just as eager to deny its existence, to obfuscate the truth, to sweep it under the rug, to perpetuate the lies and spew hatred.

"Not everything that is faced can be changed," James Baldwin, the Black author and activist wrote in his memoir *Remember This House*, "but nothing can be changed until it is faced."

So we find ourselves at that crossroads. We can face racism head on, or we can divert our eyes, excuse it away, and allow it to triumph. There's no in-between. Tolerating racism *is* racism. We all need to choose a side.

★

Since its very founding, White supremacy was consciously, intentionally, institutionalized into the underpinnings of the country, stitched into the fabric of the nation, and, thus, why it predictably and episodically manifests in American society. The only variable is how: police brutality, criminalization of Black people, in housing, healthcare and educational discrimination in so many subtle and not so subtle ways.

Nelson Mandela said, "No one is born hating another person because of the color of his skin, or his background, or his religion. People must learn to hate, and if they can learn to hate, they can be taught to love, for love comes more naturally to the human heart than its opposite."

I believe that there is something deep down inside each of us, a bogeyman of repressed fears we keep hidden—taught to us at an early age, usually in understated ways, in the images of White and Black America portrayed on TV and in the movies, in casual comments overheard in a crowd, or a heated exchanged by adults, an off-color joke, that, over time, made us question people that were different than us—like that feeling you get when you walk down a street at night and worry some-one or something is lurking in the shadows. It's only in our imagination, but it feels so real. Maybe we all have some of that in us, and it scares us that maybe we're not as pure of thought as we desire to be.

We have to—each of us—confront that monster, face our fears, tackle our de-mons, forgive ourselves and heal.

To quote Martin Luther King: "The arc of the moral universe is long, but it bends towards freedom."

Each step in that direction—no matter how small—helps to move the world that much closer to freedom for all, for, to quote King's immortal words, "I have a dream, that one day this nation will rise up and live out the true meaning of its creed: 'We hold these truths to be self-evident, that all men are created equal.'"

★

I leave you with this:

When 80-year-old John Lewis passed away on July 17, 2020 from pancreatic cancer, America lost one of the most courageous persons the Civil Rights Move-ment ever produced, a symbol of what it is like never to give up or give in, in life and in death.

In life, Lewis, the son of an Alabama sharecropper, was a central figure in the key civil rights battles of the 1960s, including the Freedom Rides and the Selma to Montgomery voting rights march. Lewis was arrested more than 40 times protesting segregation. He was involved in lunch counter sit-ins; freedom rides on interstate buses; and he was the youngest speaker at the 1963 March on Washington.

He would go on to a distinguished career in politics, first serving on the Atlanta city council before being elected to Congress in 1986. He rose in Democratic Party ranks to senior chief deputy whip, and became known as "the conscience of the Congress."

I spoke of a divided nation, of a line that has been drawn, one that separates us.

In the very same week that the world lost this great champion of freedom, Pres-ident Trump, who was rarely subtle with his racist dog-whistling, tweeted, "I am happy to inform all of the people living their Suburban Lifestyle Dream that you will no longer be bothered or financially hurt by having low-income housing built in your neighborhood." He continued, "Your housing prices will go up based on the mar-ket, and crime will go down. I have rescinded the Obama-Biden AFFH Rule. Enjoy!"

Trump was referring, of course, to an Obama-era law regarding the Affirmatively Furthering Fair Housing provision, which seeks to reduce racial segregation in the suburbs.

Make no mistake about it. This government-sanctioned, Apartheid-era, race-baiting hyperbole is ignorant and repugnant, made worse because "legitimacy" is attached ([your government] is "happy to inform you …" Could the message be any clearer?)—and is exactly what leads to situations like the pointless killing of a Travon Martin or an Ahmaud Arbery.

It represents everything John Lewis fought so hard against.

More importantly, John Lewis didn't need to tear people down. John Lewis knew how to build people up. John Lewis was a true believer who didn't need to shout his message to have it heard. John Lewis lived his message through his quiet, non-violent actions. John Lewis was a fearless hero who stood on the front lines, not a coward who hid behind a wall of lies. John Lewis was a stalwart champion in the on-going struggle for the dignity and worth of *every* human being—not just the White privileged few. John Lewis dedicated his life to building an open society where *all people* can enjoy the same rights, freedoms and justice. He wasn't closed-minded about people who brought diversity and cultural texture to our society.

In death, John Lewis left these words for others to carry on the fight.

"While my time here has now come to an end, I want you to know that in the last days and hours of my life you inspired me. You filled me with hope about the next chapter of the great American story when you used your power to make a difference in our society. Millions of people motivated simply by human compassion laid down the burdens of division. Around the country and the world you set aside race, class, age, language and nationality to demand respect for human dignity.

That is why I had to visit Black Lives Matter Plaza in Washington, though I was admitted to the hospital the following day. I just had to see and feel it for myself that, after many years of silent witness, the truth is still marching on.

Emmett Till was my George Floyd. He was my Rayshard Brooks [a 27-year-old Black man shot and killed by police in an unjustified use of deadly force case], Sandra Bland [a 28-year-old Black woman who was found hanged in a jail cell in Waller County, Texas, on July 13, 2015, three days after being arrested during a pretextual traffic stop] and Breonna Taylor. He [Till] was 14 when he was killed, and I was only 15 years old at the time. I will never ever forget the moment when it became so clear that he could easily have been me. In those days, fear constrained us like an imaginary prison, and troubling thoughts of potential brutality committed for no understandable reason were the bars.

Though I was surrounded by two loving parents, plenty of brothers, sisters and cousins, their love could not protect me from the unholy oppression waiting just outside that family circle. Unchecked, unrestrained violence and government-sanctioned terror had the power to turn a simple stroll to the store for some Skittles or an innocent morning jog down a lonesome country road into a nightmare. If we are to survive as one unified nation, we must discover what so readily takes root in our hearts that could rob Mother Emanuel Church in South Carolina of her brightest and best, shoot unwitting concertgoers in Las Vegas and choke to death the hopes and dreams of a gifted violinist like Elijah McClain.

Like so many young people today, I was searching for a way out, or some might say a way in, and then I heard the voice of Dr. Martin Luther King Jr. on an old radio. He was talking about the philosophy and discipline of nonviolence. He said we are all complicit when we tolerate injustice. He said it is not enough to say it will get better by and by. He said each of us has a moral obligation to stand up, speak up and speak out. When you see something that is not right, you must say something. You must do something. Democracy is not a state. It is an act, and each generation must do its part to help build what we called the Beloved Community, a nation and world society at peace with itself.

Ordinary people with extraordinary vision can redeem the soul of America by getting in what I call good trouble, necessary trouble. Voting and participating in the democratic process are key. The vote is the most powerful nonviolent change agent you have in a democratic society. You must use it because it is not guaranteed. You can lose it.

You must also study and learn the lessons of history because humanity has been involved in this soul-wrenching, existential struggle for a very long time. People on every continent have stood in your shoes, through decades and centuries before you. The truth does not change, and that is why the answers worked out long ago can help you find solutions to the challenges of our time. Continue to build union between movements stretching across the globe because we must put away our willingness to profit from the exploitation of others.

Though I may not be here with you, I urge you to answer the highest calling of your heart and stand up for what you truly believe. In my life I have done all I can to demonstrate that the way of peace, the way of love and nonviolence is the more excellent way. Now it is your turn to let freedom ring.

When historians pick up their pens to write the story of the twenty-first century, let them say that it was your generation who laid down the heavy burdens of hate at last and that peace finally triumphed over violence, aggression and war. So I say to you, walk with the wind, brothers and sisters, and let the spirit of peace and the power of everlasting love be your guide."

Amen.

★

CHAPTER SIX
AFTERWORD

"The way to right wrongs is to turn the light of truth upon them."

—IDA B. WELLS

I grew up in Detroit. For the first few years, in the late 1940s, my parents rented a duplex on Clairmont Street, near what would later be the site of the 1967 riots. My Uncle Sol and Aunt Fannie lived in the unit next to us. I don't remember much about it other than we had a huge front porch, and Aunt Fannie's angel food cake was out of this world.

In 1950, my mom and dad paid $21,500 for a single-family, Indian-red bricked house wedged in the middle of a quiet, elm tree-lined street just off Seven Mile Road, two blocks from Livernois—the main shopping street in town, dubbed "The Avenue of Fashion."

Behind the house we had a detached two-car garage, which took up half the backyard. In the winter we turned the other half into an ice hockey rink using 2x4s and plastic sheeting.

The house had three bedrooms upstairs with a shared bath. I had my own bedroom (brown-flocked wallpaper with illustrations of cowboys on horseback covered the walls). My two prized possessions were my red Schwinn Panther 3-speed bike and my Rawlings' brand Tony Kubek left-hander's baseball mitt (I still have the glove).

In 1952, my dad purchased a Philco black and white television. It was the deluxe model that came in a wood cabinet. I remember Saturday mornings in the knotty-pine den standing on top of the olive-green sofa with a bath towel pinned to the back of my pajama top, the TV tuned to "The Adventures of Superman" ("Look! Up in the Sky! It's a Bird...It's a Plane... It's Superman!"), as I dreamed of flying while leaping off the sofa, hoping my feet wouldn't touch the ground.

My dad's business was doing well enough that, in addition to the TV, we could afford a pink Princess telephone (a status symbol in those days and my mother's pride and joy) and even hired a "maid" (another symbol that you made it in society).

That's when Marga Nelson entered our lives. She was in her mid-30s. Born in Macon, Georgia, her family moved North during the Great Migration, as did thousands of other Black families, to take jobs in the then-booming auto industry. A lot of Black women were so rigidly excluded from good jobs that 50 percent of those who were employed in the 1950s worked as maids.

I distinctly remember my mom interviewing Marga in the living room. We were only allowed in there if we had guests visiting. My parents mainly used it for bridge parties that they held once a month on a Saturday night.

I can picture Marga, sitting in a slipper chair by the front picture window, still wearing her winter coat, with her round ebony cheeks and soft eyes, hands neatly folded in her lap, purse strap handle held in the nook of her elbow, politely answering my mom's questions. "Yes, ma'am … I sure can … Thank you." We instantly fell in love with her.

Marga was "live-in." She stayed with us Monday through Friday and went home on the weekends. My dad had a "maid's quarters" added to the basement a year before when he had it "finished" with wood paneling. It also had a wet bar. Neither of my parents drank, but that seemed to be a standard feature of all 1950s remodeled basements—well that, and a checkerboard linoleum tiled floor.

Marga's starting salary was $35 a week plus $5 "car fare." She wore a classic "maid's uniform." It was a staple then, much like when men wore suits to work—but I cringe today at the thought of her having to wear it.

When I was about ten years old, Marga left her common-law husband. I never met him. All I knew was that he worked in an auto factory and had been abusive to her for years and that she never had children of her own.

My father owned part of a furniture company in addition to his wholesale textile business, so he furnished an apartment and provided Marga with all the linens.

★

Both my parents were loving and caring, but my dad worked six days a week building his business, and my mom was busy most weekdays with her Mahjong and bridge games at ladies card rooms around town—so much of our time together was spent around the dinner table or on weekends.

Therefore, Marga had a big role in raising me. It was Marga that would take me to SS Kresge, the neighborhood "five and dime" store, so I could spend my allowance (50¢) on comics, plastic toy soldiers or, more often than not, a week's supply of candy.

It was Marga that would yell for me to stop playing stick ball in the street and come in for dinner. "Boy, you better git yourself in here!"—as my friends mocked me for having to go home. "Can't I just..." "Boy, you want me to come out there and..." "I'm coming..."

Marga was always there when I came home crying after falling off my bike or scraping my elbow trying to climb over the concrete block wall that separated the alley in back of my house from the municipal parking lot they put up a few years after we moved in. She helped nurse me to health when I was sick, and she tried to prevent me from getting into too much mischief.

When I did, though, she'd let me know it. She'd give me that look of disgust, put her balled-up hands on her hips, and say, in a voice two octaves above her normal range, "Boy, If you ain't the most, you is." I never quite understood what that meant, but I had a pretty good idea that it was not meant as a compliment.

When I was good, which was not too often, she had an infectious laugh that lit up the room. "Ha, ha, ha"—that last "ha" always coming with a snort or a grunt. When I was sad, she'd give me a hug and tell me it was going to be okay. "You better put a smile on that face, Boy."

I believe a lot of who I am today as a person, my values, the basic principles that form my belief system, came from Marga—not so much from her telling me, as showing me, through her words, her deeds, how she comported herself, the dignity and pride she showed, the way she expressed love, the way she rose above her life's circumstances.

★

In 1965, I went off to college and on to the next several chapters in my life. I would see Marga on occasion, less so when I moved East for business.

Marga was with my parents for over 40 years. When my mom and dad retired to Florida, they got her a place nearby. In the early 1990s, she moved to an apartment in Atlanta to be close to her one remaining relative, a cousin.

I would visit her whenever I was passing through town. I remember the last time I saw her, we went to a fancy Italian restaurant for dinner. We talked for hours. Mostly she wanted to hear about how I was doing and all about my family. She told me how proud she was of me and I told her how much I loved her.

It was the last time I saw her. She died not long after.

I'm glad I got to tell her how much she meant to me. Sometimes I think she's looking down and smiling. Sometimes, when I'm not so good, I can hear her saying, "Boy, If you ain't the most, you is."

I dedicate this book to you, Marga.

★

CHAPTER SEVEN
SOURCES

Books

Baptist, Edward E., *The Half Has Never Been Told: Slavery and The Making of American Capitalism*, New York, Basic Books, 2014.

Chalmers, David M., *Hooded Americanism: The History of the Ku Klux Klan*, Durham, NC, Duke University Press, 1987.

Dye, Thomas, *Rosewood, Florida: The Destruction of an African American Community*, Abingdon, U.K., Taylor & Francis, 1996.

D'Orso, Michael, *Like Judgment Day*, New York, G.P. Putnam & Sons, 1996.

Gonzalez-Tennant, Edward, *The Rosewood Massacre: An Archaeology and History of Intersectional Violence*, Gainesville, FL, University Press of Florida, 2018.

Gordon, Linda, *The Second Coming of the KKK: The Ku Klux Klan of the 1920s and The American Political Tradition*, New York, Liveright Publishing, W.W. Norton Company, 2015.

Hirsch, James A., *Riot and Remembrance: America's Worst Race Riot and Its Legacy*, Boston, Houghton Mifflin Company, 2002.

Kolchin, Peter, *American Slavery, 1619—1877*, New York, Hill and Wang, 1993.

Krehbiel, Randy, *Tulsa 1921: Reporting a Massacre*, Norman, OK, University of Oklahoma Press, 2019.

Krugler, David F., *1919, The Year of Racial Violence*, Cambridge, U.K., Cambridge University Press, 2015.

Madigan, Tim, *The Burning: Massacre, Destruction, and the Tulsa Race Riot of 1921*, New York, St. Martins Griffin, 2001.

Moore, Gary, *Rosewood: The Full Story*, Middletown, DE, Manantial Press, 2015.

Parsons, Elaine Frantz, *Ku-Klux: The Birth of The Klan During Reconstruction*, Chapel Hill, NC, University of North Carolina Press, 2015.

White Papers and Research Reports

A Brief History of Slavery That You Didn't Learn in School, The New York Times, 2019.

Black Flight: Lethal Violence and the Great Migration, 1900-1930, Cambridge University Press, 1990.

Documented History of The Incident Which Occurred at Rosewood, Florida, in January 1923; Submitted To The Florida Board Of Regents December 22, 1993.

Black Soldier, White Army, Center of Military History, U.S. Army, 1996.

Ku Klux Klan: A History of Racism And Violence, Southern Poverty Law Center, Montgomery, AL, 2017.

Letters describing the Battles of Gettysburg and Vicksburg, Manuscripts and Special Collections: New York State Library.

Lynching in America: Confronting the Legacy of Racial Terror, The Equal Justice Initiative, Montgomery, AL, 2017.

Men, Women and Children in the Stockade: How the People, the Press, and the Elected Officials of Florida Built a Prison System, Anne Haw Holt, Florida State University Libraries, 2005.

One Flag, One School, One Language: Minnesota's Ku Klux Klan in the 1920s, Minnesota Historical Society, 2009-2010.

Racial Violence and Competing Memory in Taylor County Florida, 1922, Meghan H. Martinex, Florida State University Libraries, 2008.

Reconstruction in America: Racial Violence After The Civil War, 1865-1876, The Equal Justice Initiative, Montgomery, AL, 2020.

Report: Tulsa Race Riot Disaster Relief American Red Cross, Tulsa Historical Society & Museum, 1921.

Rosewood, Florida: The Destruction of an African American Community, The Historian, 1996.

Search for Yesterday: A History of Levy County, Florida, Chapter 10, Levy County Archives Committee, 1980.

Slavery: Cause and Catalyst of the Civil War, U.S. Department of the Interior, National Park Service.

Special Masters Final Report (Equitable Claim Seeking $7.2 Million For Damages Resulting From The 1923 Destruction of Rosewood, Florida), March 24, 1994.

The Civil War, The American Yap, Stanford University Press, 2018.

The Industrial Condition of the Negro in the North, Philadelphia : American Academy of Political and Social Science, [Reprint from 1906].

The Rosewood Massacre and the Women Who Survived It, The Florida Historical Quarterly, 1997.

Transcripts of interviews with Rosewood survivors and/or their descendants from the Florida A&M University Black Archives.

Articles

"100 Years Later, What's The Legacy Of 'Birth Of A Nation'?" NPR.com, February 8, 2015.

"A Long Lost Manuscript Contains a Searing Eyewitness Account of the Tulsa Race Massacre of 1921," by Allison Keyes, *Smithsonian Magazine,* May 27, 2016.

"A White Mob Wiped This All-Black Florida Town Off the Map. 60 years Later Their Story Was Finally Told," Timeline.com.

"Ensuring the Chicago Race Riot id Not Frgotten," by Madeline Fitzgerald, *Time* magazine, July 19, 2019.

"Ku Klux Klan founded: Dec. 24, 1865," by Andrew Glass, *Policito,* 2016.

"Lynchings, 1921 Tulsa Massacre, and 8 Other Things School Didn't Teach You About Race in America," The Philadelphia Inquirer, Updated: October 24, 2019.

"Owed to Rosewood Voices From A Florida Town That Died in A Racial Firestorm 70 Years Ago Rise From The Ashes, Asking For Justice," by Margo Harrakas, Sun-Sentinel, February 21, 1993.

"Red Summer," National WWI Museum and Memorial.

"Rosewood," *The Washington Post,* May 30, 1993.

"Rosewood," by William Booth, *The Washington Post, May 30, 1993.*

"Rosewood Descendant Keeps The Memory Alive," *Orlando Sentinel,* February 1, 2004.

"Rosewood Massacre," by Gary Moore, *Tampa Bay Times*, St. Petersburg, FL, July 25, 1982.

"Rosewood Massacre of 1923 by Vicious White Lynch Mob in Florida," Iloveancestry.com.

"The Last House in Rosewood," *Tampa Bay Times*, June 6, 2018.

"Whitewashed: the Rosewood Massacre," by Erin Egloff, 540westmain.org.

Other

Various websites including RememberingRosewood.org, Wikipedia, History.com, HistoryEngine.com, CNN.Com, Tampa Bay Times, and the NewYorkTimes.com.

Author's notes: Given the events of the Rosewood Massacre occurred almost 100 years ago, information is missing and there are conflicting statements from witnesses and third parties, including several people who were present at that time or relatives of people present then who heard the stories recounted, and were interviewed several decades later—so their recall of events may not be accurate. There are also many conflicting newspaper articles about the events surrounding the massacre. I have attempted to present facts that, whenever possible, seem the most credible and supported by multiple sources. A few of the quotes in the book were constructed from interviews with witnesses and their descendants directly, or as told to them, or created to provide continuity and clarity to the work.

Throughout the book I have chosen to capitalize "Black," because the lowercase black is a color, not a person. The same holds true for "White." Also, the term "Black" is used, versus "African-American" or "Person of Color," as Black is usually defined as "of or relating to any of various population groups having dark pigmentation of the skin" or "of or relating to African-American people or their culture," so I believe it has a broader context to it. The book occasionally uses what would today be considered a derogatory and offensive racial term, so I've chosen to use "N*****" to replace the word.

My thanks to Sven Jacobson, Carol Lezell, Ibrahim Mian, and Sloan Wolf Miles for their comments, suggestions and edits on the book. My thanks also to Olivier Darbonville for graphic design of the book.

All proceeds from this book will be donated to charities, including The National Civil Rights Museum in Memphis, Tennessee, that occupies the Lorraine Motel, the site of Dr. Martin Luther King's assassination, and which puts on exhibits that "illustrate chapters of the fight for civil rights in our country in order to promote better understanding of the struggles involved;" The Thurgood Marshall College Fund, that provides, among other things, scholarships to groom the next generation of cultural leaders; and The Innocence Project, which uses DNA testing to exonerate men and women wrongly convicted by the justice system. Some proceeds will also go towards a program I founded that provides a free boxing program to underprivileged teens in the New York City area, called Strike Team.

ABOUT THE AUTHOR

Vanished is David's seventh book.

He is the author of *Fun with Hypnosis, Underbelly: The Palm Beach No One Talks About, Spank The Monkey: The True Story of Three Men, A Spanking Club and Murder, Camelot Revisited: The People And Events of 1963 That Changed The World Forever,* and *The Adventures of Murray The Wonder Dog.*